Coping with

TEEN PARENTING

Kay Beyer

THE ROSEN PUBLISHING GROUP, INC./NEW YORK

Published in 1990, 1992, 1995, 1999 by The Rosen Publishing Group, Inc.
29 East 21st Street, New York, NY 10010

Revised Edition 1999

Cover Photo by Kim Sonsky

Library of Congress Cataloging-in-Publication Data
Beyer, Kay.
   Coping with teen parenting / Kay Beyer.—rev. ed.
   Summary: Discusses the experience of becoming a teenage parent,
exploring such areas as physical and emotional changes in the mother,
basic child care, discipline, caregivers, and financial planning.
   ISBN 0-8239-3035-1
   1. Parenting—Juvenile literature. 2. Teenage parents—juvenile litera-
ture. [1. Teenage parents. 2. Parenting.]
I. Title.
HQ755.8.B49 1995
. 306.85'6 —dc20

90-8058
CIP
AC

Manufactured in the United States of America

About the Author

Kay Beyer received a BA in elementary education, a master's in education, and administrative certification from Southwest Texas State University in San Marcos, Texas. She has taught administrative theory and elementary curriculum and has supervised student teachers at the State University of New York at Plattsburgh. For thirteen of her twenty years of experience in the education field, she was an elementary school principal. As a principal, she worked with families to help them understand the difficulties of being a child and parenting a child. It is important for teen parents to know that the author herself was a teen parent. As nineteen-year-old sophomores in college, Kay and her husband, Joe, became the proud parents of a baby boy. They learned to parent the hard way and corrected many mistakes along the way. *Coping with Teen Parenting* was written to help other teen parents over the bumps. Kay still appreciates the fact that her sister-in-law was willing to give the little one his first bath.

Contents

Becoming
a Teen Parent

Maybe you have been planning to have a child. Maybe you haven't. From the moment the doctor confirms your suspicion that you or your partner is pregnant, you begin to feel just about every emotion you've ever experienced. But now you feel each one much more deeply than ever before. If loneliness is one of your feelings, you have something in common with one out of every four young women who becomes pregnant by age eighteen. If, like eight in ten teen pregnancies, your pregnancy was unintended, you may also feel confused, frightened, or helpless.

"If she's right about this then I'm in trouble," thinks seventeen-year-old Otis as he takes another order at the drive-through window. He's having trouble concentrating on remembering customer requests and making correct change. All he can think about is his girlfriend, Jade, and whether she is really pregnant. He worries because he is a responsible person and always tries hard to do what's right. To him, getting a good grade on his science test and keeping customers satisfied at the restaurant is enough to think about. But this afternoon he can't help thinking about more than that, knowing that today Jade has her doctor's appointment.

Jade jingles her keys in her pocket nervously as she waits for the results of her pregnancy test. She looks around at the other people in the clinic waiting room. It's hard to imagine that in a few months she could be one of those people with a round belly or with a tiny baby on her lap. But when the nurse calls her in and tells her that she is pregnant, Jade is not surprised. Her period is more than a month late, and she has been feeling nauseated and dizzy. A counselor at the clinic tells Jade about some of her options and gives her some pamphlets to read later. On her way home, Jade begins to dread telling the people closest to her about the baby. That will be much harder—by far— than visiting the clinic.

Who? What? When? Where?

Jade, like you or teenagers you may know, is going to become a mother. In 1996, more than 502,000 teenagers in the United States gave birth to a child. That amounts to thirteen percent of all births that year. Teens like Jade who choose to become mothers will experience dramatic changes in their lives. They must learn to compromise, to budget time and money, and to take responsibility for the care of another human being. Each mother- and father-to-be—of any age—at some point asks herself or himself, "Will I be a good parent?" The excitement of having a child is inevitably mixed up with the fear of being unable to fulfill the role of a parent.

A few months later Otis and Jade go to the clinic for one of her monthly checkups. The doctor tells them that everything is fine. Jade has been receiving more attention from her parents and friends than she has since she was a little girl. She feels a rush of joy from the sense of belonging and her awareness of the importance of the events to come. But she still has so many questions that no one seems to be able to answer. Will she finish high school? Will Otis be there for her later? To what extent can she rely on her family?

Preparation Means Planning

Although Otis has promised to stay with her, Jade, like 78 percent of mothers under age twenty who gave birth in the United States in 1997, is unmarried. Will Otis continue to care for the baby, or will he find that the responsibility is too much? Either way, Jade is lucky—she has the option to live at home with her parents, who have offered to help care for her baby. Some teen mothers are forced to live on their own because their parents don't want the added financial and emotional strain of a grandchild in the house. Other teen mothers are not accepted by their parents for religious or cultural reasons and must move out. And some teen mothers prefer to raise their children independently, without parental help.

Months after the baby is born, many of the people who are now lavishing attention on Jade will return to the normal rhythm of their lives. But Jade will remain the center of attention for at least one person—her baby.

Jade reads books like this one and may even take classes to prepare for the months and years ahead. She learns what to expect as her baby grows older. She reads about how she can help her child develop emotionally, socially, and intellectually. Maybe the sense of awe she feels and her youthful energy will help her better meet the challenges of being a young parent. She must be committed and informed enough to be able to guide and care for her child for many years after his or her birth. In this book, a young parent like you can find information about how to take care of yourself and plan for your own future, even if the arrival of your baby means putting off your own goals and dreams for awhile.

Support Systems

Jade prepares for her baby. What does this mean? Buying baby clothes? Having a baby shower? Stocking up on formula? Yes, but it also means much more. If Jade decides to live at home, she must discuss how the baby will fit into her parents' lives. How will her parents help out with childcare and money? Maybe she will have to work out a budget to make sure that she is contributing enough to her child's needs. Most probably she will need to plan a schedule that eases her responsibilities but also gives her parents time for themselves.

By reading books like this one, teen mothers can find out about the many resources available to them. Teens who don't live with their parents will need to know how to line up help elsewhere. They may need to ask for financial assistance, as well as advice on nutrition and parenting. By the time their child is born, they may have found out that they had to request help from a relative, even if they didn't want or need to before. Every mother, no matter how able or strong, needs a lot of help for the first few weeks after her baby is born.

The Baby Arrives

Now Jade's baby is born. What at first seemed like an end-less string of clinic appointments went by very quickly. Life has changed dramatically. During the past eight months, Jade has planned a daily schedule with her parents, lined up financial resources, made shopping lists, and arranged to take time off from school. But Jade has not prepared for everything. Each day brings new questions, and Jade is frequently exhausted. In fact, she often feels overwhelmed. Her baby is a separate being and caring for it is incredibly exhausting. Jade never imagined what it would be like to have to wake up so often during the night. Sometimes she can't figure out why the baby cries. The new stress she feels is already creating difficulties in other parts of her life. Every day Jade stays at home while Otis and her other friends go to school. Otis visits almost every night after work, but the days are long and often lonely. It can be difficult for Jade to see her mother so much, and it is frustrating to listen to her mother's advice when she'd like to be more independent.

What's in This for You?

Parenting is definitely a new adventure for you. Much of the time spent being a parent is a wonderful, exhilarating experience. You witness "firsts," such as a smile, rollover, tooth, and crawl. You share events with family and friends. But it's often a struggle too. No one who has been a parent will say it is an easy job. To cope with parenting, you will need basic parenting skills; a network of support including friends, relatives, nonprofit agencies, and the government; an understanding of the difficulties you will face just because you are an adolescent; and a plan of action to overcome these known obstacles to teen parenting.

The next chapter of this book explains the realities of teen parenting and lists the five obstacles that a teen parent must overcome to be successful. Later chapters cover child care basics, child development and communication, and health and nutrition. The final chapters are dedicated to the parent and answer questions about health, setting new goals, birth control, and where to get more help from books, on the Internet, and from nonprofit organizations. No matter how frightened, lonely, or confused you may feel, remember that there are always people who can help you. With preparation, planning, and some help along the way, your child-rearing years can bring happiness and health to both you and your child.

Basic Facts for Teen Parents

Teen parents are in the stage of life called adolescence, a time of rapid growth and development. The teen parent is not only growing up, however, but also coping with the new responsibilities of being a parent. To cope with parenting, the teen needs to know:

1. How to meet the needs of an infant or child. Parents have the job of helping their child become the best he or she can be. They want to provide a safe and loving environment in which the child can grow and learn. Because parents care, questions about *what, when, where,* and *why* often arise. These questions are not unique to teen parents. Parents of all ages, whether first-time or not, share many of the same concerns. All parents have doubts about what to do and wonder if they are doing the right thing. Most minor mistakes are harmless to the long-term development of the child, and most questions about basic child care can be easily answered in a book. One of the purposes of this book is to provide teen parents with information about basic child care that should make routine decisions easier and lessen some of the doubts.

2. How to find support for and solutions to difficult problems. All family situations are different. Some

7

problems are more challenging and not so easily solved. Some life-threatening emergencies require fast and clear-cut answers. Both new and experienced parents at times need expert or emergency advice or help. Part of this book serves as a guide to knowing when and where to go for the help you need. The book may suggest asking questions of experienced parents, including the grandparents of the baby. If the problem is difficult or dangerous, the suggestion may be to seek expert help from such specialists as medical doctors, counselors, or social service workers.

3. Why parenting is more difficult for teens. Teens who enter parenthood face many challenges. Teens are in a stage of life during which they are still growing, learning, and slowly becoming independent. Becoming a parent will not make the teen an adult, nor will it automatically give him or her the skills needed in life. That will take time and experience. Since the experience has to come "on the job," teen parents face some additional challenges.

4. How to plan to meet the special obstacles that face teen parents. As this book depicts the ordinary wonders and problems of being a parent, it also attempts to prepare teen parents for tackling the difficulties unique to them. It focuses on the positive aspects of being a teen that can help him or her meet the demands of parenting.

The Advantages of Teens Being Parents

The youthful energy and enthusiasm of teenagers is a plus for the job that has to be done. Teens generally can handle the long hours and remain excited about the job of parenting. Teen parents also have not had as much time to become "set in their ways." They probably will be more spontaneous in dealing with their child and more flexible in adjusting to change. A young adult's ability to "go with the flow" of things will help greatly in parenting.

In studying teen parents, however, researchers have found five obstacles that most must face. An understanding of these difficulties combined with careful planning can be very helpful. Let's preview the five obstacles that may be roadblocks to a younger parent's success. As you read, think about how the obstacles apply to your personal situation. The five factors unique to teen parents that make parenting tougher—but not impossible—are these:

1. A limited number of people are available to share the responsibility of parenting with the teen parent. The majority of teen parents are single; a second parent is not available to share the responsibilities. Friends no longer lead the same lifestyle as the teen parent, as most will be continuing with their social and school or work life. The teen's parents may not realize how much support a youthful new parent needs. Even if they know the teen needs help, they may not have the time or energy to give it. Some may not know how to help, and others may refuse to give it. The new grandparents may not want to have to deal again with the problems of parenting. Consider your personal situation. Who can you count on to help? Who is available to fall back on when the going gets rough?

2. All humans develop emotionally and socially through stages, maturing from infant to child to adolescent to adult.

9

Teen parents take on the important adult responsibilities of caring for an infant. At the same time they must grow and develop as adolescents. All humans going through adolescence must overcome the normal teenage insecurities, oversensitivity, instability, and feelings of rebellion against adult authority. The social and emotional growth of the adolescent years can be confusing and difficult to handle. Adolescence is a time of seeking independence and freedom, but it is also a time when teens still need to turn to their parents.

Teens search for themselves, wondering about their future as independent adults and asking themselves "What do I want to be?" and "What do I want to do?" During their search, teens can act very erratic—agreeable one day, disagreeable the next. Their self-esteem (how they feel about themselves) and body image (how they see themselves) change with their moods. At a time when change in mood and desires is frequent, there is a certain intolerance for others. It doesn't take much for parents to be seen as "being in the way" of a teen's push for freedom. In response, teens rebel against the authority of their parents.

At the same time, teens still require love, nurturing, and guidance from their parents or others. This process of growing and maturing is difficult enough for a teenager who does not have the added responsibilities of parenting, so imagine the challenges for the teen who is a parent. Parenting may interfere with meeting the adolescent developmental tasks and forming mature relationships with parents and others.

3. Fertility levels of teen parents are higher than those of other age groups. When a person starts out having a child early in life, research shows that she or he tends to have more children than average and has them sooner than other people. Having one child early probably means having another one soon. The already overburdened teen or young adult who is in pursuit of his or her life dreams and is a parent will have an even harder time reaching goals with each additional child.

4. *Life plans change or must be postponed.* Teen parents in the pursuit of their life dreams are handicapped by the needs of their new family. The educational potential of a teen is not met, teen parents often do not finish high school, and college is forgotten or postponed. Because teen parents often lack work experience and education, job options are few. The teen parent generally is financially strapped to a low-paying job and/or support from parents or welfare.

5. *Family structure and lifestyles change.* The delivery of the first baby leaves the teen parent tense and bewildered. With the birth of the baby, the grandparents assume a job in addition to the difficult one of parenting their ever-changing teen; they must now give additional support to that teen as he or she attempts the hard job of parenting. Living arrangements also change. At least half of all teen parents, even if married, continue to live with their parents. In addition, the arrival of the baby demands financial changes for both the teen and the grandparents. The days of free spending of allowances or money earned come to an abrupt end. Teen parents need financial support but usually feel inadequate in the role of provider for their baby when they are supported by others. The lack of money and the cost of good child-care limit teen parents' freedom to come and go. Grandparents also feel the financial burden.

Obstacles—Planning to Avoid Them

Chapters one and two have made you aware of many of the questions, doubts, and obstacles that may arise in your new role as a teen parent. If you know the roadblocks that challenge new parents—and especially teen parents—you will have a better chance of overcoming them.

You have taken the first step toward achieving your goals and dreams in life by reading chapters one and two. The second step in preparing to become a parent is the learning and planning stage. A section at the end of each of the remaining chapters is devoted to helping you better understand the potential obstacles to teen parenting and to providing suggestions for planning to overcome them. Remember that the information in these sections is factual and is intended to improve your chances of succeeding. It is in no way meant as a put-down of adolescents or teen parents. It is a means for you to find out why other teens have or have not been successful as parents. You will have the opportunity to learn the easy way—from the mistakes and successes of other teen parents.

As you read the remaining chapters, be honest with yourself. Identify the problems you are facing now or expect to face. Seek answers and solutions. Plan for your future and the future of your child. Then read chapter sixteen to begin putting your plan in writing and into action.

The Basics of Caring for a Child

Where Are the Instructions?

A new baby does not come with a set of instructions, and many new parents have not had the experience of caring for an infant. The little one is totally dependent on you, the parent. The baby will be demanding and require attention. He or she comes with the sucking reflex. You must supply the breast or bottle. A baby cannot sit up or walk, and its head will flop if not held carefully. You provide the support. As with any new experience, you will need to ask questions or get help from someone who has already been through the process. One way of getting a good start with your new baby is to have an experienced mother share the basic care of the baby for the first few days. You have just gone through your first delivery. You will probably need some rest, and you may be feeling concerned about being a first-time parent. All mothers, including first-time teen mothers like you as well as experienced forty-year-old mothers of four, benefit from having help during the first few days with a new baby. Do not hesitate to ask for help.

Holding

Babies must be held with care, but they are not fragile. Until a baby can control and hold its head up, you provide the support. Hold the baby carefully with one hand supporting the head and the other the "bottom." Holding the baby gently and securely close to your body keeps the baby safe and builds his or her trust in you and the new world. You give the baby a feeling of love and security.

Diapers—Cloth or Disposable?

When choosing which kind of diaper is right for your baby, take into consideration your budget, your time, and your baby's comfort. Also think about where you live. Do you have easy access to laundry machines? Are stores nearby? Then research and experiment. Find out which diapers best "fit" your baby and your finances: cloth (either self-wash or through a diaper service) or disposable (either regular or biodegradable). Test both types with your baby. Which type makes him or her happier and less fussy? Can he or she tell the difference?

Cloth diapers are soft, all-cotton, and highly absorbent. They are easy to adjust and you never have to worry about plastic or tape tabs chafing against your baby's skin. Do use care with safety pins, though. Cloth diapers breathe well but do not wick (soak up) liquid away from the skin as well as synthetic fiber disposable diapers, so you will need to use nine or ten cloth diapers each day on your infant.

Cloth diapers may be cheaper in the long run. Once you purchase them, you will have the diapers until your baby is toilet trained, which could be two or more years away. But do you have to wash them, or will you have to use a diaper service? The cost and availability of diaper services varies greatly, so research is necessary. Using a service saves you time because you pay the company both to wash soiled diapers and to deliver clean diapers to you. Once considered the most environment-friendly option, cloth diapers are not necessarily good for the environment today in areas suffering from drought, such as the southwestern United States. Also, commercial and home washers and dryers use very large quantities of energy, and washers use even greater amounts of water.

Disposable diapers are made of synthetic cloth and plastic and come in a variety of sizes and brands. They absorb waste well. Because disposables wick moisture away from the skin, your infant will need only about seven changes each day to stay comfortable. Some babies do not like the plastic linings and tape tabs that hold these diapers in place. They may fuss if the chafing makes them uncomfortable. Disposable diapers may be more expensive than cloth. The total cost of all the diapers you use will continue to add up as your baby grows until he or she is toilet trained. But you will never have to wash disposable diapers, which saves you time. Disposable diapers are a significant environmental problem, however. Because they all end up in landfills, disposables are particularly damaging to the environment in areas with high-density populations, such as the large cities in the northeastern United States. Some are marketed as biodegradable because they may decompose more quickly than regular disposables after being thrown away. But according to sanitation experts, most landfill covers do not allow garbage to decompose naturally. Because of this, when changing a soiled diaper, no matter what kind, flush all stool down your toilet rather than dropping it into the household trash.

Bathing

Babies should be kept clean for reasons of comfort and health. Babies should be bathed daily. After the navel cord comes off, real baths are in order. Also, the baby should be cleaned thoroughly after each feeding and spit-up and as part of diapering.

If you feel unsure about bathing, you are not alone. Most new parents feel the same way. Ask the baby's grandmother or an experienced friend to help with the first bath. The newborn will most likely not be happy with the first experience, and your inexperience may not make it better. You will learn by watching and helping, and the baby will be in experienced hands.

Think . . . Talk . . . Plan the Baby's Bath

Preparing for a baby's bath makes it easier on both you and the baby. You will be less tense and the baby will enjoy baths more. Examine your schedule and the needs of your household to plan a time for the baby's daily bath.

⤳ *When?* The usual time to bathe the baby is after the first morning feeding. Don't forget that the baby needs a fresh diaper and sometimes a change of clothing before that morning feeding. (Chapter four discusses reasons why you might want to schedule an evening bath.)

16

⮑ **Where?** Choose a warm room and a safe, clean place for the baby's bath. A fancy bathing and dressing table is not necessary. For the "real" baths after the navel cord drops off, you may use an inexpensive plastic baby tub or even a clean kitchen sink or large bathroom or dish basin. The main concern is that the tub or sink is clean for the baby's bath and washed carefully for later kitchen use. A low table, even a card table, makes an excellent dressing table.

⮑ **Getting ready.** Prepare the water. Check the temperature carefully. A bathing thermometer is nice, but with experience your elbow will work just fine. Get all necessary items ready before you start the bath—soap, washcloth, towel to place the baby on, towel for drying, diaper, diaper pins, any lotions used, and clean comfortable clothes.

⮑ **How?** Until the navel cord comes off, do not put the baby in water. Give the baby a sponge bath, a thorough wash with a soapy cloth and then a rinse with clear water. As with the "real" bath, wash and rinse the head and face first, then the body. When the baby begins baths in a tub, support the head with one hand. Use your other hand for washing and rinsing. Always avoid splashing water in the baby's face.

⮑ **Safety.** Never leave the baby unattended while bathing, drying, or dressing him or her. Make sure the drying space is big enough.

↬ *Fun and learning.* Talk to the baby as you give the bath. Allow the baby to hold the washcloth when he or she is old enough. Bath time can be an exploring time and fun time with water. Add toys to the bath when the baby learns to sit.

Feedings—Breast or Bottle?

Breast-feeding is the least expensive option, but there are four other conditions that make a difference in the decision to bottle- or breast-feed your baby:

1. The baby receives some natural defenses from breast milk and forms a real closeness to you.

2. Your availability for breast-feeding makes a difference. Mothers who work or attend school may have a problem scheduling feedings. However, some babies will take a bottle if the mother is going to be out for one or two feedings. The bottle can contain formula or the mother's own milk. (A mother who is breast-feeding can express milk for use while she is away. Care must be taken with the storage and freshness of the mother's milk.) Breast-feeding can be scheduled for just before the mother leaves and as soon as she returns.

3. The amount of milk you can produce makes a difference. Some babies will take a bottle when extra milk is needed.

4. You may have personal feelings about breast-feeding that make you choose to use bottles. You may feel

that you will lose personal privacy by breast-feeding your baby. If you are not sure about breast-feeding, you may want to try it. Let family and friends know that you want privacy by excusing yourself to another room. When visiting friends, just ask to use another room. However, many mothers feel comfortable placing a diaper or light blanket over the baby and mother's breast while nursing. They remain in the company of family or friends. The covering also helps some people who might feel uncomfortable seeing a mother nurse a baby.

Think . . . Talk . . . Plan

Breast-feeding the baby for at least the first month or six weeks may be beneficial to his or her health. How will it fit in with your schedule? How much privacy do you think you will need? How can you prepare relatives and friends for your need for privacy? How will your family react to having you nurse the baby in their presence?

Burping

Babies who are bottle-fed suck in some air. To lessen the amount of air, hold the bottle at an angle that keeps the nipple full of milk. To release the air bubbles from the baby, burp him or her. Place the baby face down on your lap or over your shoulder. If your baby tends to spit up, place a diaper or towel on your lap or shoulder. Pat or rub the baby's back gently to release the air bubbles. Some babies need to be burped during feeding to make room for their meal. Others can wait until they finish a bottle.

Scheduling Feeding

A baby should never have to cry long because of hunger. Be prepared and try not to make your baby wait too long. Any schedule you try should be flexible. Some babies may need to eat every two hours at first. As they get older, they will want to eat about every four or five hours. Meeting babies' needs makes them feel secure in their world.

Feeding Solid Foods

Follow your doctor's advice and your common sense in giving your baby solid foods. The doctor will be observing the following to advise you on adding solid foods to your baby's diet: (1) your baby's weight gain; (2) the maturity of his or her digestive system; and (3) any tendency toward allergies.

Sleeping—Bedtime? Naptime?

All babies are different. Babies with colic have trouble going to sleep and remaining asleep. (Read more about colic in chapter four.) Some infants sleep through the night from the very beginning, whereas others wake up every two hours. Your job is to make the baby as comfortable as possible. You must keep in mind that the baby has needs that must come before your need for sleep. To survive the sleepless nights, remember that this stage in your child's life will end. He or she will begin to sleep through the night. Babies do grow up and out of each stage.

How much sleep does a baby need? A healthy, comfortable, and happy baby can answer that. He or she will sleep as much as necessary. He or she will tend to be awake at certain times of the day. A new baby may sleep from feeding to feeding. As the baby gets older, the naps will occur twice a day and then once a day. Unless you have a very good reason, never wake a sleeping baby. If a friend or relative comes to see the baby and the baby is asleep, let the baby sleep. The baby's routine of napping at certain times of the day should not be broken. You and the baby may "pay later" when he or she is too tired and fussy to go back to sleep.

CAUTION: Babies begin to push themselves around very early. Never place a baby on a bed or couch to sleep. He or she may scoot off and onto the floor. Placing a baby on the floor on a blanket or quilt is safer, though be sure that he or she is protected from pets and dangerous objects and is out of the way of busy adults.

Think and Talk About

A thirty-one-year-old first-time parent shared a story of her baby's first overnight visit to the grandparents. The plane and car rides went smoothly. However, the mother and child had to share a trundle bed. The three-month-old baby was placed on the bed for his morning nap. He slipped behind the bed and became stuck. Both mother and baby were frightened. Fortunately, the baby was not hurt. However, pulling the screaming, frightened baby from behind the bed was as upsetting to the mother as to the baby. She decided to return home after only two days of her two-week visit.

21

Playtime—Free or Guided Time?

Guided and shared playtime is loving and learning time. New skills can be taught to the baby and practiced together. But babies and children also need free time to explore, learn, and practice "old tricks." Allow the baby to play alone. Playing-alone time should be provided when the baby is most comfortable, rested, and secure.

Clothing and Equipment Needed for Basic Care

The following list is provided as a guide. Check off items as you make purchases, are given items in usable condition, or receive gifts for the baby. Because of the expense of baby items and the many items needed, you do not want too many duplicates. When you have the money to purchase items, stick with the list before you add things that are just "cute." Keep the list handy if you have a baby shower or for when people ask, "What do you need for the baby?" Show them the list. They can purchase something needed in their price range.

Think . . . Talk . . . Plan . . . List

Diapers
_____ **cloth**
Two to six dozen, depending on how often you can wash (one dozen even if you plan to use disposable diapers)
—diaper pins

22

—diaper pail for soaking

—waterproof pants or diaper wraps

_____ **disposable**—a starter supply. (Watch for sales and use coupons, but do not buy too many small ones. Remember that newborns double in size in three to five months.)

Clothing Other Than Diapers

For the following items, the magic number is from three to six of each. How many your baby needs depends on how often you can wash.

_____ **outerwear**—dresses, diaper suits, shirts/blouses, and diaper pants (often given by friends and family at showers or handed down from baby to baby)

_____ **nightgowns with mittens on sleeves**

—with drawstring ends for covering feet

—without closed ends

_____ **undershirts**

_____ **caps**

_____ **socks and booties**

_____ **blankets**

_____ **waterproof sheeting** to cover even a plastic-covered mattress

_____ **waterproof/quilted pads**

_____ **sheets**

_____ **sweaters** (depending on the season)

_____ **snowsuits** (depending on the climate you live in)

Feeding Items:

_____ **bottles and** ____ **nipples** for formula, water, and juices (also may be needed for additional feedings for breast-fed babies)

_____ sterilizer
_____ container for mixing formula
_____ measuring spoons for formula
_____ bottle brush
_____ nipple brush
_____ tongs (to pick up hot bottles from sterilizer)

Equipment:
_____ baby bed
_____ infant seat
_____ infant carrier (seat and carrier may be combined)
_____ automobile infant seat

Miscellaneous:
_____ thermometer
_____ absorbent cotton for applying ointments/oils
_____ soap
_____ towels
_____ washcloths

Nice but not Necessary/May Need Later:
_____ bath thermometer
_____ pacifiers
_____ bottle warmer
_____ infant nail scissors
_____ baby lotion
_____ diaper rash ointment
_____ stroller

Other Items:
_____
_____
_____

Think and Talk About

Special Obstacles for Teen Parents Concerning Basic Child Care

As pointed out in chapter two, teen parents face unique obstacles. The *Think and Talk About* sections at the end of each chapter, including this one, were written to help you tackle these difficulties. One of the five obstacles we discussed in chapter two will affect your plans for basic care of your baby:

Family structure and lifestyles change. If you live with your parents or other relatives and depend on them for support, you may have to adjust your plans for baby care. Your purchases, use of space, and schedule for the baby must be planned with the needs of other family members in mind. The choices you can make may be limited. The family budget may not stretch to include all of the items you want or need for the baby. Many of the decisions you make about space and when it is used for the baby's care will be based on the needs of the entire family. The usual activities such as leaving for school or work must go on. The evening hours may be quiet times for your family. How can both the baby's and the family's needs be met? Talk, talk, talk. Talk before and after the baby comes. Plan together. Give reasons for your requests. Share the information you have learned. For example, explain why a large space is necessary for drying and dressing the baby. Suggest more than one place. If your choices are not acceptable, ask for suggestions. Try to adjust to final decisions. Keep in mind that your parents have had at least one baby to raise. Remember, everyone is making some adjustment just because there is a new baby in the house.

As you work with your family, you will probably make some adjustments to your first choices for baby care. The infant's schedule may have to change. The baby may need to wait for his or her bath in the kitchen sink until after the family's breakfast time. The baby's bath may have to be shifted to the evening to help preserve family quiet time. (Some babies tend to cry in the evening; a bath may quiet him or her.) You realize that the card table often is used for other activities, so you can't set it up permanently for a bathing and dressing table. You listen to a family member's suggestions for a bathing and dressing space that will work just fine. As you make adjustments to meet not only your needs but also those of the baby and other family members, you are taking giant steps in getting along with others. You are learning to relate to the needs of others in a mature way.

To help with the budget, work from the list of items for basic baby care. Look for bargains and sales. Baby items do not have to be new—just clean, safe, and in usable condition. Buying or borrowing used equipment such as a carrier or stroller is a good idea. And because babies grow so fast, many clothes can be handed down. These are just some of the ways that you can meet your baby's needs and help with the family budget at the same time.

Body Talk:
Communicating with
More Than Just Words

LISTENING . . . Responding

You will notice that the word "listening" is in capital letters whereas the word "responding" is only in small letters. That reflects how important listening and understanding are to the communication of ideas, feelings, and attitudes. Communication takes at least two people expressing themselves and listening to each other. *A message is communicated only when the listener correctly understands the meaning of the message being given.*

Your baby is trying to tell you something when he or she cries and fusses. If you jump in with an early response, you will probably give a bottle when he or she may only need to be held to feel secure and loved. Listen and watch for clues to what your baby is "saying."

Messages from You to Your Baby

From the very beginning you are giving messages to your baby. When the baby cries "I need," you take care of the need. You are saying, "I am here for you." With each move you make, you are saying "You can count on me." "Hungry? I will feed you." "Wet? I will change your diaper." "Lonely? I will be with you." "Unhappy? I will comfort you."

27

Messages from Your Baby to You

And of course, the baby works hard to tell you what his or her needs are. Your baby will use crying in the beginning to send messages. Later he or she will be able to smile and coo. Finally, specific sounds, words, groups of words, and sentences will come, and you will continue to respond. Parents and babies give two-way messages from the very beginning.

Open eyes and ears to understand the messages. Just listening to sounds and words and ignoring the clues of a baby's, child's, or even an adult's body language can be misleading. Think of a time when you talked with someone and heard one message, but the redness of the person's face, a revealing grin, or the sadness in the eyes hinted at something different. Facial expressions of the mouth and eyes offer clues. Body movements such as placement of arms and shoulders and body stance provide additional information. Sometimes a person's very straight face without any expression tells you that what he or she is saying is a joke. Laughing eyes can also give away the true meaning of the message. Then you know the person is just kidding. Remember when you were a child and your parent folded his or her arms and looked at you sternly? You knew you were in trouble. You must continue to listen with your ears and your eyes.

Listen to your baby with your ears. Different kinds of sounds from babies carry different messages. A baby uses various types of crying or sounds of happiness and contentment to

28

express his or her needs, wants, and feelings. As a parent, you must listen carefully to understand the message so that you can give the needed response. Within the first month, you will learn to recognize what the baby is trying to "say" with each kind of cry or other sound. A cry can mean anything from "I want to fuss now" to "A diaper pin is sticking me." Crying at the top of his or her lungs will alert you quickly to a problem. By gurgling and smiling as he or she lies in bed in contentment, the baby looks and sounds fine. He or she is saying, "Things in my life are okay."

"Listen" to your baby with your eyes. Understanding each other comes from more than words and sounds. Listening carefully is not enough. Watching for body clues is the very backbone of your understanding of your baby. The baby gives you a clue with his or her entire body. He or she may even seem to reach for you at times with his or her entire body. At times he or she may draw arms and legs in to show pain. Expressions on a baby's face also give different messages. A fussy baby's face will show only minor displeasure. If the baby shrieks in pain, his or her face all red and scrunched up, you will know to be alarmed. A red face, tears in eyes, and a quivering mouth send different silent messages to you.

Baby receives messages with eyes and ears. There are clues for the baby in everything *you* say and do, too. Babies receive clues from both the words and the body language of parents. Parts of your body express how you are feeling and what your attitudes are. The expressions on your face, fast movement of your body or the waving of your arms, the loudness and sharpness of your voice, and the speed of your talking add meaning to what you are saying. What messages have you been sending to your little one?

Think and Talk About

When people, including babies, send messages, they are trying to give information, share ideas, and let others know how they feel. You get the real message using your eyes and your ears. You are ready to respond. What is the real message this baby is getting? *The mother says to the baby, "You poor, sweet darling. I do love you." As she talks, she slings and throws the toys out of the way, using a fast, gruff manner. A tired frown shows on her face.*

Practice watching for clues as you communicate with your baby and others. At times you may have snapped at a friend, your spouse, a relative, or your baby when you did not feel well. Your words said one thing and your snapping meant something else. Being aware of how you approach others, including the baby, will help. Talking to someone about how you feel can relieve some of your frustrations. If you find your approach to the baby is too harsh or uncaring, you probably need a little time away. Tell someone. Ask for time to relax and regroup. Take care of yourself. When you feel better about yourself and your situation, the baby will know because your smile will show.

Crying Sends the First Messages

You have a baby in the house. Expect some crying! A crying baby is not always saying "I'm hungry." Babies cry to sound off about being hungry but also to tell you such things as I am thirsty, cold, hot, uncomfortable, in need of burping, or just lonely. A lonely baby may cry just to get to hear your voice, see your face, experience the pleasant feeling of your patting his back or your comforting arms holding him or her gently. Some little ones fuss just before they fall asleep. More active babies tend to cry more and with a louder message. The message is not necessarily more urgent. They just "let off more steam" and spend more time telling their new world that they have arrived. Quieter babies may spend more time lying awake and sucking their fist for pleasure. We often hear parents say, "He's such a good baby. He hardly ever fusses or cries." If your baby is one of the more active sound-off babies, the "good baby" may sound wonderful after a tiring day. But keep in mind that both babies are in the normal range. One is just more active and not content to lie quietly and look at the world. The fussy baby actually may move out into the world faster and learn faster.

Some babies who sound off may have real reasons. The baby may be in pain. He or she may be neglected—not fed enough, wet most of the time, or not receiving enough love or comforting. The baby is in need of immediate care.

How do you know what your baby's crying means? If you hear every cry as hunger, you will have an overfed baby. (See chapter nine on nutrition and the overfed, overweight babies who tend to have weight problems as adults.) Remember, crying is your baby's first means of communicating to the world. With experience you will learn the difference in his or her cries. You will learn to distinguish between fussing and a real need for attention. Until you figure your baby out, try everything. Check the diaper first. Did he or she just eat and now has an air bubble? Maybe a diaper pin is sticking. Did the solid food make the baby thirsty? Think of all possibilities before giving an early or extra feeding.

Does your baby choose early evening to sound off? Evening is probably the time of day when you are most tired and the household is the most active. You are involved with each family member's arrival home, cooking the evening meal, or getting ready for the next work or school day. What can you do if your baby chooses this time to be fussy and seek attention? There are solutions to the problem. Try placing the baby near you as you work and talk to him or her about anything. If you are resting, place the baby on the bed or couch with you. Visit with baby as you rest. He or she may just need some attention.

Try switching your baby's schedule and making early evening a special time. Schedule a feeding or bath time. The baby will have to choose another less important family time to fuss. If you decide to use evening as bath time, make the experience even more special. Use it as a "getting to know you" time for the other parent or another family member. Make it a time for family members to enjoy the baby together. Bath time can become fun time and play time for the baby and family. As bedtime gets closer, the pace can change into a relaxing, soothing, and reassuring time for the baby as a family member rocks or reads to the baby. The baby gets to spend time with at least one person who has not had to answer to each and every call or cry for the entire day, and the parent who cares for the baby all day gets help with the baby's care. Evening time can become enjoyable for everyone.

When should I become alarmed by my baby's crying? If your baby seems to be in pain, call your doctor. If your baby cries too much, ask your doctor about it during a regular visit. He or she may recommend a formula change or more or less to eat. The doctor may also tell you that the baby has colic.

What is colic? What can I do about it? Some babies have colic during the first three or four months. How can you tell if your baby has colic? The baby's message is more than just a late afternoon or evening fussiness. The screaming after a feeding will give you a loud, clear message. If your baby is experiencing the pain of colic, he or she will cry hard and show pain by drawing arms and legs in. His or her face will turn red. The little tummy will seem tight to the touch. The baby with colic feels hard cramps.

Unfortunately, not much can be done. But knowing that colic is the problem helps you to avoid becoming overly alarmed. It is reassuring to know that colic is a common problem in young babies and will be outgrown. The baby's digestive system is immature. With age and the maturing of the digestive system, colic finally tapers off.

However, as a parent who has experienced the

shrieking of a baby from sundown to nine or ten o'clock at night will tell you, the experience is just as painful and trying for the parent as for the baby. If possible, the care of a baby with colic must be shared to avoid parent fatigue. A parent may become tired and irritable during long sessions of trying to soothe the baby. He or she must work hard not to show annoyance. If you are the parent of a baby with colic, you probably are tired. The crying comes when you need to be cooking the evening meal, want to have a calm enjoyable evening with other family members, or need sleep. As you try to soothe the baby, you will probably think about the parents you know who say that their baby rarely ever fusses. You must remember that your baby is in real pain. You have the job of making him or her as comfortable as possible. You must be patient and comfort your baby. Until the baby outgrows the problem and the pain, you must be ready to help each night.

If your baby has colic, you can expect a lot of advice from grandparents, friends, and neighbors. You will hear cures ranging from putting socks on the baby's feet to feeding more. Some people may even think that the baby is spoiled and that you should ignore the crying. Just listen patiently. Even put socks on the baby if it makes some adult happy. They are only trying to help. Remind yourself daily that the colic will go away as the baby grows older. Your baby is not stubborn, naughty, or spoiled. You will not spoil the baby by trying to keep him or her as comfortable as possible during the painful times. Holding, patting, and soothing the baby may not take the pain away, but it is necessary for the baby to feel safe and secure. He or she will know that you do understand.

Next Your Baby Will Smile, Gurgle, and Try Sounds

How does this start? It takes you—smiling, laughing, touching, and talking. From the very beginning the baby studies your face and sounds. Your voice soon stills his or her crying. When you move in close, he or she reaches for you with the whole body, the little arms and legs wriggling in excitement. To keep the excitement and show love, you smile and talk. It doesn't matter what you talk about; the baby listens, enjoys, and learns. The baby mimics the smile, makes some sounds, and practices sounds discovered accidentally. "Conversation," that funny "cradle talk" that imitates the flow and rhythm of language, is the beginning. The baby "talks" by learning to vary sounds and pitch. There are highs and lows and probably even some shrieks of joy in the attempt to tell you something. The only message you get is that you have a happy baby. You should not stop answering, however: Communication is two-way. Continue to talk, talk, and talk.

At about six months your baby will begin to repeat sounds. The sounds may not even be useful to the language he or she will learn to speak, but they do give practice in repeating sounds. Sometimes he or she attempts to echo the sounds you make and hits on one. But there are no real words yet. The baby talk is mixed with bubbles and other fun lip noises. Baby may even begin to use certain sounds instead of crying to call you. You should respond enthusiastically. Let the baby know that you will come when called, and he or she will use the sounds to call again and again.

Then the first real words come. You have repeatedly called out the words Daddy or Mama and given the words meaning by your actions until the baby knows what the words mean. Now he or she repeats it. By his or her first birthday, your baby probably will have up to a dozen real words to use in communicating with others. He or she will hold lengthy conversations with a mixture of invented words, real words, and an imitation of the flow and rhythm of language. You will attempt to interpret by listening and watching for clues. He or she may soon wave to gesture bye-bye and then add the word. You will understand and help by repeating the word. You will say bye-bye and wave many times. Your baby associates the sounds and meanings. He or she begins to understand the meaning of words.

The baby was able to think and feel before he or she could talk. His or her world expands through the use of language. Now he or she can communicate those thoughts and feelings. Real companionship comes for the child through communication. The baby soon can tell others where it hurts and can let you know when he or she is afraid or lonely. Parents can more easily manage a child who can talk. A parent can call the little one back without going to him or her every time. A baby can be told why he or she cannot to do something: "The stove is hot." Your child also now has a new defense with others. He or she can defend with words rather than crying, hitting, or running away. Your baby begins to use words to remember past events and to anticipate future ones. Talking actually becomes his or her favorite "sport." Pattycake and peekaboo become favorite games. Baby and parents enjoy the fun of communicating and playing together.

You might ask about your quiet baby at this time. Yes, you may have one who was content to lie quietly instead of crying. But when it comes to wanting to express ideas and to tell something, the quieter babies get just as involved. As a human being, your baby is a social being and will want to share ideas and feelings. The first words and signals are just the beginning.

Communication and Your Baby's Emotional Growth

A baby's first years determine his or her future ability to relate to others and to the world. His or her emotional well-being is established by the caregivers. First, the parents are the communicators of how the baby will feel about him- or herself for life—his or her emotional well-being. Second to the parents are the people chosen as temporary caregivers, such as other family members, baby-sitters, and day care workers. People and environment will have a lasting effect on the child. Babies and children who are loved and nurtured and live in a trusting environment grow up to be emotionally healthy adults. Those who are neglected or abused in the early years will deal with the lack of nurturing or abuse for years to come. The medical profession now recognizes forms of mental illness that have their beginnings in the first years of a child's life. If a child does not bond (form a close, trusting relationship) with the person or persons he or she must rely on, emotional problems may arise later.

Finding out how important you are to your child's future emotional well-being may frighten you. The good news is that your job is simple. The sharing of warmth, love, and pleasure in day-to-day living will give your baby strength to face the world. Keeping your baby away from any environment of violent behavior, nervous tension, harsh bossiness, or abuse is another key factor. Careful choosing of caregivers for your baby is important. Select people who meet your expectations and desires for your baby's emotional growth. (Never hesitate to remove your child from the care of someone, even a relative, if necessary.) Building an atmosphere of love and caring around your baby in all of his or her relationships with people will help. Model and teach your child to have and show caring and respect for other people. That caring and respect will be returned to him or her from others.

The Parents' Job: Modeling Good Speech

Smiling, laughing, touching and holding, soothing, listening, talking, and asking questions are important caring messages. Talk! Talk! Talk! from the first day. Talk about anything or nothing. Read to your baby. Read children's books, a magazine article, or a parenting book to your child. Use your best, soothing voice. Model good speech. You get to read something you are interested in. At the same time, the baby hears the language and the caring tones of your voice.

Allow your child to speak like a child. Most mispronunciation of words will improve with time. You need only repeat the word correctly for the child. You are modeling correct speech. He or she will copy you and outgrow most problems. If the child continues to have problems with a certain word or sound, you may want to make a "silly" game out of working on the word or sound. If your child stutters when excited or upset, wait patiently while he or she talks. Do not force the child to perform for others by talking, reading, or singing. Do not tease. If the child is still having difficulty at age three, consult your doctor or public school for testing. You can find out if your child will outgrow a speech problem or get a recommendation of a program to help. Some schools have preschool speech programs for children who have not outgrown a speech problem.

Do not encourage baby talk. A baby may have his or her own words for some things. They help him or her fix meanings to certain objects or actions. These are bridge words used until he or she learns enough words to communicate in the language of the parents. To parents and friends, some of the special sounds or words are cute and funny to hear. Because of that, some parents encourage the use of baby-talk words long after the baby can give them up. The use of these words keeps the baby from moving on in learning the language. The immature sounds used to communicate as a baby should be dropped. (Baby talk may reappear when a new brother or sister arrives. It will go away just as easily.) Continue to provide your child with a good model.

Another problem arises as the child grows older. Sometimes a child repeats some of the "bad" words heard from other children and adults. Many times adults reinforce the use of these words by smiling or laughing. Some parents even ask the child to repeat the words for others. Some brag about the child using these words. The child is being set up by the adults. Teachers, other adults, and even the parent will be upset if the child repeats the words at the wrong time. It may sound cute at home, but at religious services, school, or even the grocery store, the use of inappropriate language can be embarrassing.

Think and Talk About

Special Obstacles for Teen Parents Regarding Communication

Two of the five obstacles that may cause problems for teen parents have an effect on their communication with others: **Teen parents are in the adolescent stage of human growth and development, and their family structure has changed.** The family structure changed with the arrival of your baby. The family became a three-generation family. You are a parent to the baby, responsible for its care and guidance. But you are also an adolescent child to your parents, who are still giving you support and guidance.

With adults, your responses may become negative. Your parents show concern and give advice. As an adolescent, you are oversensitive to advice and may view it as criticism. In fact, at times you respond defensively to any advice. You may have heard the message before and do not want to hear it again. It could be about something that really bothers you. Or maybe you don't want to be reminded. You may also feel that your parenting skills are being attacked. These thoughts and feelings interfere with the message. The message, even if helpful, is pushed aside and ignored. To receive the necessary messages you must open your mind as well as your eyes and ears. Try to listen, for the sake of your child and your future. To fully understand the message, watch for clues. The message on the speaker's face may show real caring and an understanding of your situation. It may be saying, "I care and want to help." Reach for independence while reaching out to others for help. Independence will come gradually, and you will grow up. Slowly, you will need less and less parenting.

With a baby, you may let feelings from your daily frustrations or feelings about your life situation keep you from listening and responding. You may even show anger. You are tired of being called on, and baby's calls may seem like nagging. You see the baby as just another person asking for more than you can give. The question of spoiling may enter your mind. When frustrations of the day change how you feel and how you approach your baby, *stop and read* chapter twelve—Child Abuse: Hurt That Lasts a Lifetime.

Now is a good time to work on building future communication with your child and others. By starting early, when your child is a baby, you can build your future "give and take" with your child. When he or she is a teenager or young adult, the love, trust, and caring shared now will carry your relationship. By sharing positive ideas, feelings, and attitudes with your child and allowing him or her freedom to give you respectful feedback, you lay the foundation for future communication. Part of growing and maturing to adulthood is learning to relate to adults. Build a positive relationship with your child and others by:

41

1. Listening without unnecessary interrupting.

2. Looking for clues to the person's real message.

3. Choosing words that do not cause misunderstandings. (Sometimes a word means something different to you than it does to the listener.)

4. Allowing for feedback from the other person on his or her understanding of your message.

5. Asking questions and allowing questions if the meaning of the message is not clear.

6. Realizing that people relate what is being said to their own personal life experiences and to the trust and confidence they feel in the person speaking.

Development

Children learn and grow in different ways and at different times and rates. Your child may talk before his or her older cousin does. The first word may come before the baby cuts a tooth, or he or she may have four teeth before the first word is spoken. Your child may walk long after a neighbor's baby of the same age. Books and charts can only give age ranges of the usual times for learning and growing. The three areas of growth are *intellectual growth* (learning to do something), *social and emotional growth* (relating to other people), and *physical growth* (using the body for play and movement). You will learn about the usual rate of growth in each area, but use the information wisely. Do not push your child before he or she is ready. Do, however, provide the necessary experiences and nutrition for your child to develop in the normal range. Keep in mind as you guide your little one that babies learn through all the senses: touch, taste, smell, hearing, and sight. If your baby was premature at birth, was a low-birth-weight baby, has been ill, or is disabled in some way, expect goals to be met later than in the normal range. Talk with your doctor or a social worker about getting special help for your child if needed.

You need to know when your child can be expected to accomplish a new skill for three reasons. It will give you an idea about how well your child is growing and developing: Is he or she within the normal range? It also will help you decide what skills to help your child learn. And knowing what to expect next from your baby will make parenting more interesting.

This chapter will guide you through the social, intellectual, and physical development stages of babies and young children. For information on physical growth (height and weight gains), check with your doctor. Keep records in a babybook or notebook for all three areas of growth and development and for weight and height gains. Even parents with one child lose track of their child's accomplishments and growth. Why keep records? Doctors and schools may need and ask for this information later. And, of course, there is a "just for fun" reason. When your children are older, they will be interested in "When did I?" and "How big was I?" and you will want to remember and share their important milestones with them.

THE MILESTONES

One to Six Years
Your child will change more in the first six years than in any other five-year period in his or her lifetime. Use the age ranges given in this chapter to track the growth and development that takes place, but keep in mind that there are individual variations. All children are different.

The Newborn—The First Month
All babies look different, even at birth. However, newborn babies, regardless of ethnic origin, tend to be fairly red

and maybe even somewhat purplish in color. At first, the head seems more long than round and has a few bumps. Within a few days of birth, the head will become rounded. The infant is born with a soft spot on the top of the head covered by a tough membrane for protection. Do not worry. Normal care in holding and caring for your baby will not hurt the soft spot. The soft spot allows for growth of the skull and will cover over at about eighteen months. When the baby comes home from the hospital, the umbilical cord is still attached to the navel; it will drop off in ten to fourteen days. Babies' eyes are dark blue or gray and change color gradually. A few babies are born with brown eyes. Because of the mother's hormones before birth, both boys and girls sometimes have swollen breasts, which go down in a few days. For the same reason, boys often have enlarged testicles, which also return to normal size in a couple of weeks. Girl babies may even have slight bleeding from the vagina a few weeks after birth. This is nothing to worry about. The newborn:

- Has a natural rooting and sucking reflex; feeds every two-and-a-half to four hours around the clock; settles to three- to four-hour feedings in a few weeks

- Is alert for only three minutes per hour on average unless he or she is hungry, feeding, wet, lonely, fussy with colic, or just uncomfortable

- Eats, sleeps, and cries to call you

- Flinches at a light and may follow it in an irregular way but sees little or no detail until about three weeks old; can focus for a while at three weeks to respond to your expressions and follow objects

⮑ Hears and responds to loud noises; can be startled even by small noises; is upset by angry voices; likes the sound of your loving voice

⮑ Tastes, smells, and pushes things out of the mouth using the tongue

⮑ Lifts head off the bed for a few seconds

⮑ Moves about a little by hunching and squirming if placed on the tummy

⮑ Has clenched fists

⮑ Reaches out to you with the whole body for comfort and support; likes to be held surely and firmly

⮑ Spits up because of the loosely closed channel from mouth to stomach (different from vomiting, which is with force and in large amounts and is a sign of illness)

⮑ Hiccups following feeding

One to Four Months

No longer a newborn, your baby will become more active, grow more rapidly than at any other time, begin to build trust, and reward you with smiles when you do "the right thing." The "do-something" baby:

⮑ Holds head more steadily; holds it erect for a few minutes; then learns to control it

- Begins to relax hands

- Needs to look, feel, and handle; learns to use touch, taste, smell, hearing, and seeing senses

- Studies things that move; by two or three months watches objects that move from one side of head to other; later can follow more distant objects at different positions

- Has a steady weight gain of as much as an ounce a day (about a pound a month)

- Holds a rattle very tightly, with feet kicking and both arms waving; drops the rattle and does not seem to care; is more interested in attention from you than in the rattle

- Stops crying at the sound of your voice

- Reaches with entire body—feet, tummy, mouth, and eyes—for someone who approaches

- Uses mouth not only for sucking but also for feeling, puckering, and making endless faces

- Omits at least one night feeding; moves toward sleeping through the night

- Explores things in relation to the body; discovers hands and feet; enjoys rolling around; likes being in new places; at about three months can bring hands together and soon can pass objects from one hand to the other

↪ Holds legs up at three to four months; can push back when feeling pressure on bottom of feet

↪ Eats some solid foods, thinned with milk at first (added one by one on doctor's advice)

↪ Enjoys mobiles and crib toys; curiosity grows fast

↪ Can look to source of a sound and follow; at four months hears as well as an adult

↪ Is awake about half the time

↪ Develops self-esteem from new learning and praise given for that learning; practices new skills over and over again

↪ Enjoys watching activities

↪ Likes excitement and games

↪ Enjoys being outside

↪ Listens to rhymes; enjoys picture books

Four to Eight Months

Baby has become more content and less demanding. The brain is developing fast as a very alert baby, interested in everything, uses his or her mind to explore and learn. Moving through his or her world to explore becomes a full-time job. Baby is playful and busy. Keeping up with this baby takes more energy and understanding. The middle-months baby:

⇨ Learns something new nearly every day through ordinary experiences; is curious, wants to see what is happening in the world

⇨ Sleeps through the night by four to five months

⇨ Mimics attitudes of the family at about four months

⇨ Giggles and laughs

⇨ Uses maturing body; develops new skills and combines old ones; can be propped up

⇨ Sits at about six-and-a-half months

⇨ Crawls to get around (uses hands and knees, tummy, or feet and hands)

⇨ Pulls up to stand

⇨ Stands at about seven-and-a-half months

⇨ Walks as early as eight months or as late as fifteen months

⇨ Knows what is going to happen next; shows by adjusting posture to the next activity

⇨ Gets bored and fussy if left alone for lengths of time

⇨ Repeats own sounds by six months, makes own conversation—delightful cradle talk; changes pitch from high to low, first repeats vowel sounds and then consonants, uses voice, not words, to tell something; uses certain sounds to call out; makes bubbles and sounds using saliva; understands some of what is said; sooner or later says real words

⮑ Plays with people to learn to get along; plays with things to master body

⮑ Holds rattle for lengths of time and looks for it when dropped; enjoys movement and color of bright toys hung across bed; enjoys squeaky toys

⮑ Uses fingers separately; likes to scratch on surfaces

⮑ Enjoys games and water play; plays games such as peekaboo and hide the toy or bottle

⮑ Is shy and develops a fear of strangers at about seven to eight months, whining and pushing them away; needs time to get used to them

⮑ May develop fears

⮑ Is interested in you talking and reading to him or her

⮑ Is teething; tooth may appear at around six months

⮑ Likes to look at other people's eyes

⮑ Becomes more childlike in feeding, eating solid foods and finger foods; has three meals a day by four to eight months; may give up formula or breast milk for regular milk; when able to sit, will join family for mealtime; learns to experiment with own feeding

⇨ Has nap schedule set at two naps, morning and afternoon

Eight to Twelve Months

Your active and delightful baby prefers to be the center of attention. He or she shows a distinct personality, wanting to be part of everything you do. The toddler, a busybody but a delight:

⇨ Walks and may even run; begins with crawling and creeping; stands and moves from one piece of furniture to another; begins to walk at eight to thirteen months (may be later for some); walks like a tightrope walker with hands out; falls often, lurches, and staggers; begins to develop balance; no longer falls to get down

⇨ Has had to watch the world around him or her; now can explore it

⇨ Is sensitive to anger of others

⇨ Gets into everything; needs more supervision

⇨ May remove clothing; can unbutton

⇨ Begins to use words, then action-word combinations, then sentences

⇨ Helps adults with work by following them; mimics their actions

Age One—The Sum of First-year Growth and Development

Intellectual Growth

- ➷ Says words like: hi, bye, Mama, Dada

- ➷ Has sounds for other words

- ➷ Knows mother, father, and other members of the family

- ➷ Distinguishes strangers; determines trust

- ➷ Can spend half-an-hour alone with playthings

- ➷ Is responsive to and absorbed in every detail of the world

- ➷ Anticipates with delight every step of the daily routine

- ➷ Mimics dancing; makes own music

- ➷ Loves games with noise and elements of surprise; can join in and mimic

Social and Emotional Growth

- ➷ Has felt some or all of the emotions experienced in a person's lifetime; decides which people to trust

- ➷ Is more interested in people than toys

⇨ Recognizes how others feel when someone is not pleased with his or her actions

⇨ Catches the mood of those around him or her

⇨ Feels deep attachment to people who care for him or her

⇨ Shows affection

⇨ Likes to be around other children; supervision of group play is still needed

⇨ Is fun to be with

Physical Growth

⇨ Is one-and-a-half times birth length

⇨ Has tripled birth weight

⇨ Controls head, trunk, arms, and legs

⇨ Uses fingers and thumb to pick up tiny specks

⇨ Drinks from a cup

⇨ Is constantly active and moving; gets around rapidly, creeping and crawling and perhaps even walking

⇨ Crawls up stairs and comes down a few

⇨ Gets in and out of furniture

↩ Has a wake, sleep, and eat pattern

↩ Has four to six teeth

↩ Enjoys physical play and roughhousing

↩ Is choosy about foods; eats coarser foods from seven to nine months; picks up finger foods

Ages One to Three—From Toddler to Child

As a toddler, your child is independently active and out-going. He or she begins to match new physical abilities of crawling, climbing up, and walking with ideas and energy that do not seem to end. It is hard trying to keep up with your child. Your little one has changed from quiet and manageable to suspicious, curious, and bossy. The only other time a child works so hard to establish independence is during adolescence. This is a time for sharing closeness with caregivers, exploring the world, and practicing the physical skills that take the toddler step-by-step to childhood. The child:

↩ Begins to understand that he or she is a separate person; establishes self as an independent person (this is the negative stage); wants to run own life and may have temper tantrums.

↩ Is increasingly attached to mother; works toward independence; moves away, crawling, creeping, and walking; pulls away and then runs back faster; has complicated life of wanting to "run every-thing" without mother.

- Rejects father and grandmother but behaves better for them than for mother.

- Resists being laid down because it interferes with the wish and need to be up; even diapering takes extra effort; bedtime becomes a hassle.

- Uses thumb and finger together.

- Changes posture gradually but greatly; balance and coordination improve; feet point straight, knock-knees straighten out, and feet no longer tilt.

- Lives dangerously; it is the age of accidents for this independent investigator; has no sense of danger; is adventurous and curious; may tamper with the forbidden; cannot be left without supervision.

- Needs quiet time before bedtime; is fretful or whiny for attention; becomes a jailbreaker from bed; bounces up after being put to bed and during the night.

- Is independent, crotchety, and cross; less easy to feed; plays with and investigates food; changes behavior from meal to meal; makes some "on purpose" messes; may refuse to chew; eats with fingers before using spoon; wants to feed self; becomes a fairly complete but not a neat feeder of self.

- Needs less food in proportion to body size.

- Cuts down on nursing and bottle-feeding as use of cup increases; may be weaned by a year;

sucking may continue—thumb, pacifier, or blanket and thumb.

↪ Begins toilet-training at eight to ten months, usually after walking; may need to wait to start at eighteen months; trains between two and three years of age. Training is not complete until the child has control, when he or she can hold it and let it go and has the sound or word to let the parent know "I have to go." Bladder control occurs between eighteen months to two years, when there is more time between voidings. Night dryness comes at about three years.

↪ Begins chatterbox stage; by second birthday has up to 300 words; repeats over and over. Greatest addition of words comes during this period. Words used to express action; has own words to bridge between child and adult talk. Plays with sounds and words long after talking. The late talker may be as late as three years old.

↪ May stutter until talking is mastered.

↪ Plays with everything with purpose; learns through tasting, touching, smelling, hearing, and seeing.

↪ Manages body—to shove and push, hit and grab, lift and throw, climb and jump, pinch and squeeze, poke and break off; gradually improves until movements are effortless by age four or five.

↪ Begins imaginative wordplay at eighteen months; continues to age two-and-a-half or three; learns how it feels to be somebody or something else; a block of wood becomes a car or the child may become a car himself; plays out real-life roles with copying and gestures; uses voice inflections; releases anger; relives experiences that are upsetting, mysterious, or enjoyable.

↪ Plays everywhere from a box to a clothes hamper; needs area with room to play and store things.

↪ Gets involved in a greater variety of experiences; is interested in things to do.

↪ Can work with parent to put things away.

↪ Has fun outdoors, sitting on grass watching ants, picking up pebbles; can have hours of happy play in a sandbox with cups and spoons to dig; later makes roads, tunnels, castles.

↪ Needs a watchful adult to keep him or her in fenced area.

↪ Has some friends; may be provoked by other children; may need closer supervision; may bite and hit or be the victim; refuses to share and considers everything "mine"; needs guidance to learn to share.

↪ Walks alone but may still drop to all fours to move faster in the beginning stage of walking.

↪ Shifts from absorption in self at about two or three; begins a thorough study of people and things.

⤴ Teases about doing things; may move toward a forbidden item or place to get attention.

⤴ Accepts water and juices from a cup at six months or older; gradually weans from the bottle.

Four–Five–Six
At these stages, the child:

⤴ Wants to learn to do things right

⤴ Wants to know how things work; where they go, and what fits into what; tries out everything

⤴ Likes being read to; "rereads" stories using the pictures as clues

⤴ Leaves behind the imaginative world for reality; joins the real world

⤴ Uses body effortlessly; rides a tricycle; moves on to bike with, and then without, training wheels

⤴ Begins formal learning at school between ages five and six

The Parents' Job—Helping the Child

Parents are very important to their child's growth and development. Whether the child reaches the fullest potential depends on the parent(s). You provide the *love, care, experiences,* and *freedom* necessary for a child to learn and do his or her best in life.

Nurturing love gives a baby the security to move out into the world. A loving parent spends time and gives attention to his or her little one. There should be daily, regularly scheduled playtime/learning time. Learning, of course, is child's play. Learning takes place as the parent smiles, laughs, talks, sings, and reads to the baby. Learning takes place using the objects and toys the parent selects for the little one.

Basic care is important to learning. A wet, hungry, or tired baby does not have time to learn. He or she has to spend too much time being fussy. The baby must be kept comfortable and reasonably happy. The parent should react to the baby's requests and needs immediately. (See chapter three for information about basic baby care.)

That same mom or dad will keep the baby close as he or she goes through the day working and playing. The parent is providing the child with experiences in the world. The baby gets a chance to watch the day-to-day happenings of the family. He or she is allowed to visit with friends who come to call, including adults. The early learning months are not spent in a crib or playpen wondering who or what might be out there in the world. The baby is freely allowed to touch and handle, look at, smell, and taste things of interest. The baby gets serious about learning because he or she has the opportunity to have experiences with people and things. The baby is stimulated by all that happens to keep investigating and exploring. The baby puts things in his or her mouth. He or she feels, drops, and works on any object shared by the parents. What looks like play is purposeful learning for the baby. The play even takes the parent down to baby's level as moms and dads lie on the blanket with their children to talk or crawl as they play.

A baby develops into his or her best from the experiences he or she has. If you talk to your child, he or she learns to talk. The parents model and the child watches and listens. The child learns by imitating, repeating, and practicing the new skill. As the baby learns from the experiences, the parent gives praise for learning. When the little one succeeds at even the smallest learning task, the parent shows excitement by smiling, laughing happily, handclapping, or saying "Yea, you did it!" The cheering tells baby what he or she needs to hear to continue wanting to explore and learn. The parent is saying "You worked hard. It wasn't easy, and it was important. I'm proud of you." The parent's enthusiasm and interest go a long way in producing more learning.

The parent provides not only experiences and stimulation through play but also the *freedom* to explore. To give your child the freedom to explore, provide him or her with a safe place to play. The inside and the outside play areas are safe. Objects that could hurt the baby, might damage other objects, or might be damaged in play are removed from the play world, as are items of value. The baby is now free to explore without someone always saying no. (See chapter ten for ideas on childproofing a play area.)

Think and Talk About

From the information you have read about learning, decide which baby has the best opportunity to be the very best he or she can be.

Baby Gottfried

"I wish it wasn't such a big problem to go out with my friends once in a while," thinks Shawa late one afternoon as she arrives home. Shawa lives with her mom, Penelope, and her eleven-month-old son, Gottfried. Each day Shawa stays at school until one-thirty, when she usually comes home to feed her son and put him down for a nap. But today she hangs out with friends at the library after school.

While cleaning up, Penelope says nothing as Shawa walks into the living room. There Shawa finds Gottfried awake and lying alone in his crib. He is fussy and ignores the toys scattered around him. Shawa checks his diaper, which is soiled—like always. "I'll wait to change him till his bath. That way I'll have some time to study," thinks Shawa as she tries to come up with an evening plan that will include dinner, a bath for the baby, and her home-work. Gottfried cries more loudly as his mother lifts him from his crib. In an attempt to calm him, Shawa offers him her breast milk, which he takes for a few minutes. Soon he pulls away and makes a choking sound, then coughs. He has gas. Shawa tries to com-fort the baby for a few minutes, but nothing is work-ing, so she places him back in the crib and goes to the kitchen to set up the high chair. "I'd like to eat too, but it's so messy when Gottfried eats, so I won't," thinks Shawa. She takes some solid food from the refrigerator, heats it, and returns to the crib in the other room to get her baby. Still crying, Gottfried arches his back and resists the high chair. Shawa decides to feed him from her lap. Most of the food ends up on her new jeans, which makes Shawa think, "Forget about having him try to drink from a cup today."

With no secure place for Gottfried in the kitchen, Shawa must bring him back to the crib once again, even though it is not bedtime yet. She returns to the kitchen to clean the dishes and prepare the sink for bath time. "It's almost six and I haven't done my homework yet!" says Shawa aloud to herself as she sponges the counter.

"Maybe you should have come home after school," says her mom. Shawa knows better than to start a fight, but she wishes that she and her mother could work out some kind of agreement. When the bath is filled, Shawa brings Gottfried back to the kitchen and quickly washes him. A splash in the face sends her looking for a towel, and Gottfried is alone for a few seconds. After the bath, Shawa dresses her child in his nightgown and then gets her math book. Gottfried plays alone on the floor while Shawa studies and Penelope watches television.

Baby Jesse

"I don't know what I'd do without my break this afternoon," thinks Stephanie as she walks through the front door of the house she lives in with her mom, Mina, and her eleven-month-old daughter, Jesse. On Wednesday afternoons between two and four o'clock, Stephanie hangs out with high school friends. Two months ago Stephanie's mom agreed to watch Jesse at this time. While Stephanie is at school, Jesse stays at a day care center and Mina works. The

Wednesday schedule has not been an inconvenience to Mina, since Jesse usually naps while Stephanie is out. And when Stephanie returns home, she has a routine already planned out. Today is no exception, even though she has a math test tomorrow.

At 4:05 PM Jesse stirs in her crib, and soon she cries out for attention and for a new diaper. Stephanie checks the diaper, which is soiled. She requires only a few minutes to set up the kitchen with everything she needs for the changing: a high chair with yesterday's newspaper on the floor below, a couple of towels and plastic bath toys, and a kitchen table clear of clutter and food to serve as a changing area. She also places Jesse's secure chair on the counter near the sink so that they can "discuss" their day while they wash the dishes "together." Then Stephanie gets Jesse. She changes the diaper and lets the baby wear a cloth diaper during dinner. Then Jesse watches her mom wash the dishes from the countertop. "Today I talked about Blakeley College with my English teacher, baby," says Stephanie as she sponges the sink basin. Jesse gurgles in approval. It's time for the high chair and dinner. Stephanie spoon-feeds her little one and places a few drops of water in a practice drinking cup for Jesse. The baby grasps the cup and turns it over immediately. "Good try, sweetie!" says her mom, who raises an adult-size glass filled with iced tea to her lips. "Hmm, I love to drink from my cup!" she says. The baby grabs her cup and turns it upside-down once again, even though Jesse is actually trying to follow her mom's lead.

Before feeding is over, Stephanie starts to fill the sink with warm water. It is just after five o'clock and *the baby blows bubbles happily in anticipation of bath time. A rubber ducky and colored rings are nearby as Stephanie removes Jesse's shirt and diaper. Soon Jesse comfortably splashes in warm water. Mom excites baby about another routine, their own made-up game of "push the duck." The yellow toy glides across the water from mother to baby and back again. Jesse can hold herself up, but towels are close at hand in case of an accident. As long as Jesse is in the sink, her mom never leaves her side. After bath time Stephanie sits with Jesse for some holding, rocking, and face-to-face smiles. Stephanie offers her daughter some formula from a bottle and then relaxes with her child. Once Jesse falls asleep she will be in her crib for the entire night, so Stephanie plans to finish her homework and visit her own mother, too.*

Teaching Your Child

A child's first learning comes from the parents' teaching and modeling. Research by educators tells us that there are steps to teaching a child a skill. There is a pattern to how a child learns. You can guide new learning with the same steps educators use in the classroom. When teaching your baby or child a new skill, show excitement to *get his or her attention to the task. Tell the child what he or she will be able to do after you work together.* Talk about how to do the activity while you model it for the child. You are *giving the child information and showing him or her how the task is done.* Next you will share the experience with the child. You are *checking his or her understanding as you work together.* Sometimes you find that you need to show him or her again. If the child is ready, he or she can begin to *practice with your guidance*. Never allow your child to practice a skill incorrectly. It is harder to learn the right way if he or she has to unlearn the wrong way first. When your child has learned the skill, *provide the time and the materials to practice on his or her own*.

Example: The baby is repeating sounds, and the mother wants to help the baby learn to say and understand her first word. The word is DaDa. The mother chose the thirty minutes before the father was to arrive home from his job each day to work with the child. She repeated the word each day. When the father arrived home she showed enthusiasm and called him over and over—DaDa, DaDa. The child began to realize that DaDa meant her father. Father responded each time the mother called his name. The activity was continued each afternoon. The mother would "call" DaDa. She would repeat the word for the baby. The baby watched and touched the mother's lips as she spoke. Then the child began to try to mimic the mother's sounds. Mother continued to repeat the sounds correctly and praise the baby as she tried. She smiled and laughed as the two of them made it into a game. The mother continued to show excitement as the baby attempted to repeat the sounds. As the baby came closer to repeating the word correctly, the mother showed more excitement. The child knew she was doing better. Then one evening, when the father arrived home, the baby was repeating the word DaDa. He picked her up and answered laughingly "What?" each time she called his name. The baby continued each day to call DaDa.

Sometimes she called too often. It was time to move ahead to another word and meaning. The parent had guided the child to new learning. The fun and satisfaction the parent felt from the child's accomplishment was the payoff for a teaching job well done.

Think and Talk About

In the example, did the parent:

- ↪ Get the baby's attention and excite the child to learn?

- ↪ Tell (or show) the child what she would be able to do after working together? (By calling the father, she would receive an answer.)

- ↪ Model the right way to say the word?

- ↪ Give the child information and show her how DaDa could be called?

- ↪ Check the baby's understanding as they worked together?

- ↪ Let baby practice with guidance?

- ↪ Give baby the time to practice on her own?

Yes, the parent in this example used the seven simple steps to help the baby learn a new skill. Think through the steps and decide how you would teach a toddler to put together a simple five-piece puzzle.

How About the Teenage Parent and Baby's Learning?

Think about the positive things you bring to parenting. You are enthusiastic and have a lot of youthful energy. You are flexible and willing to try new things. You are optimistic and believe that if you try something, it will work. With these assets you should have no problem exciting your baby about learning. Your high energy and flexibility will make crawling on the floor to play with your baby acceptable. That same energy will give you time for housework, work or school, and baby's learning. Your optimism will carry you through some of the constant "repeating" necessary for baby's learning. Playing with baby will be something you both will enjoy.

Having read the first part of this chapter, you have the basic information about your baby's growth and development. You can use the information as background to talk with family, friends, and the baby's doctor about your child's milestones. You have the vocabulary to discuss your baby's progress or lack of it. No one knows your baby as you do. If there is a problem, you will be the first to know. If you don't have the solution to a problem, ask and follow advice. Get help if needed. Make wise and practical use of your understanding of the stages of your child's growth and development.

Let's look again at the five obstacles to teen parenting:

➯ *A limited number of people are available to share the responsibility of parenting with the teen parent.* Your child's basic care and learning will be almost totally your responsibility. Time will have to be used carefully to get everything done. If you are a single parent living away from home and your baby attends a crowded day care center or has no outside-the-home learning, you carry total responsibility. You now have the knowledge to teach your child.

Possible solutions: If possible, share the care and teaching of the child with the other parent, even if the two of you do not live together. If you live at home, start talking early with your parents about your ideas on joint responsibility for baby care and household duties and about the information you have learned concerning human growth and development. If you need to work, consider working at a mother's-day-out or day care center to help with finances and be close to your baby while he or she learns. The baby gets to be with you and in a group situation. The opportunity to play and relate to other children is important. Often an employee receives free childcare or a reduced rate along with salary.

↪ **Teens are in the adolescent stage of growth and development.** You are inexperienced in many aspects of childcare. Keep reading, asking questions, and learning.

↪ **Fertility levels are higher for teens than for humans of any other age group.** Teen parent statistics reveal that those who start having children early have more sooner. If you multiply the time needed to assist one child in learning and developing by two or three children, you probably do not have that much time. Divide the time you have

68

to spend with your child between two children. Even though children learn from each other, two children get only a portion of the parents' time. Plan carefully for additional children.

Possible solutions: Planned parenthood means making a decision to postpone additional children, spacing them carefully, or limiting the number you will have. Contact your local Planned Parenthood group or your doctor about ways of preventing unwanted pregnancies. Planning ahead will help you avoid making "after the fact" decisions.

↪ **Life plans change or must be postponed.** If you postponed your plans to finish school, get a college degree, or have a certain career when you became pregnant, you have given up a lot. Use your time wisely to give your child a good start, then start again on your dreams.

↪ **Family structure changes.** If you are not living on your own or with the baby's other parent, you are probably part of a three-generation family. It is difficult having two roles in the family. You are your parent's adolescent child and your baby's mother or father, somebody's child *and* somebody's mother or father. Decisions you make about parenting may be different from those of your parent(s). Your parent(s) may share the care of the baby while you work or go to school. Your parent may not be as concerned about the baby's development as you are. The baby may spend hours in the playpen while your parent is doing housework. You are concerned about his or her learning and development. However, if it were not for the care given, you could not continue your education or work to help with financial needs. Talk over your baby's care with the person. Where you live, who the other family members are, and your relationship with them do make a difference. Teen parents often do not have a choice. Share what you have learned about parenting with those who help care for your baby.

Self-Concept and Self-Confidence

How do you see yourself? How do you feel about yourself? Can you say "I like myself! I can and I will"? Do you view yourself as a valued and valuable human being? Do you believe in yourself and your abilities? Are you satisfied with who you are and where you are going in life? To feel good about yourself, you need to work on being able to answer yes to each one of those questions. *If you feel good about yourself* (self-concept), you will be more successful in helping your child feel good about him- or herself. *If you are sure of yourself* (self-confidence) you will find it easier to help your child be sure of him- or herself.

What should you do to improve your self-concept? To start, you need to develop good, sharing relationships with the people around you. Chapter four, Body Talk: Communicating with More Than Just Words, offers suggestions on improving the way you relate to others. Second, you must recognize your accomplishments and have a plan for the future. You are beginning to feel successful as a parent. Think of the positive things you are doing as a parent. Just reading this book means that you care about your child and are taking steps toward becoming the best parent you can be. Your self-concept will improve as you plan for and take action toward building your future. Chapter sixeen is designed to help you plan and move steadily toward your life goals. Last, but just as important, you should take care of yourself. You have needs that must be met. Chapter fourteen, Parent Care: Your Own Needs, will help you examine and plan for your individual needs. Your answer will become "I like myself. I can and I will."

Your Child

There are ways that you can help your child build his or her self-concept and self-confidence. Your child will know and be able to say "My parent loves and believes in me." From that foundation he or she can say "I like myself. I can and I will!" His or her self-concept stands on being able to say "I like myself." His or her self-confidence for facing the world stands on being able to say "I can and I will." How do you build those good feelings for your child? Here are eight suggestions to be used again and again.

1. From the beginning, hold, talk to, pat, hug, and kiss your baby. The building blocks for your child's future self-confidence and self-concept begin the first time he or she is placed in your arms. By showing and continuing to express love and affection, you are telling your child that he or she is worthwhile. As a result, he or she will begin to feel worthwhile and important.

If your family has not shown you love openly with words, holding, and touching, you may find it awkward at first to do so with your own child. You may think that touching is always sexual. It is not. It can be a normal way of sharing affection. Starting early, while your child is most dependent on you, will help. Demonstrating your love with words and with touching soon will seem natural. If you hold, hug, and kiss your child as a baby, toddler, school-age child, and teen, the two of you will continue to share the same kind of warmth when he or she is an adult.

Holding, rocking, and patting are also very important for forming the bond between parent and child. Bonding is creating the sense of belonging—a "falling in love" that happens between parent and child. The mother probably will be the primary person involved in the beginning. If a father is present, his ability to bond with the baby is equally important. He should immediately begin to get to know his baby and share in giving the baby the feeling of being important and belonging. Yes, fathers can hold, hug, and show love too. For many, it will come naturally; for others, it may take some adjustment.

As a child grows out of the baby stage, both parents should look for opportunities to continue to show love. Just because the child is too big to fit comfortably in your lap does not mean that he or she is too old to share love through touching. Continue to tuck your child into bed and to sit close with your arm around the child's shoulders. A pat on the head, a back rub, and hugs and kisses should be a part of his or her growing up. Showing warmth does not take extra time when done as a part of everyday life. It can be done in the car or while watching television or playing a game. Starting early with your baby will make it usual and expected.

2. Make time for your child. You may live in a household with many people. There may be children in your household other than your own. You may have more than one child. You may work or go to school. The amount of time you give your child changes as: (a) additional children come into the family; (b) your child grows out of the dependent stage and demands less and less of your time for everyday care; and (c) your outside-of-the-home duties and responsibilities increase. You will have to plan or make time for each child. An infant will demand a lot of time, whereas an older child will be less dependent and less demanding. It is still important to spend time with him or her, however. Quality time alone may have to be arranged daily or at least weekly for the older child.

How do you find the time? Use driving to appointments, going to the grocery store, or short walks as sharing time. Hold hands, walking and talking along the way. Make arrangements when possible to take only one child along.

What do you do in this special time? Let your child talk about things of interest to him or her. Make it a conflict-free time. Do not use the time to nag your child about past behaviors. It is a time to enjoy each other. It is a time to feel close. The special times together continue to say to your child "You are loved. You are wanted. You belong."

The time you spend with your child pays now and pays later. The parent who makes time to listen while a child is young will be the one whom that child may be more willing to talk to during the teenage years. He or she will be more comfortable in coming to you for help. The two of you have made a habit of sharing time, interests, and problems. Parent and child sharing has become the usual, the expected.

But what about spoiling? A child can never be spoiled

by having his or her needs met. A baby needs contact with his or her parent(s) to feel safe and secure. These good feelings are necessary to emotional growth. When a baby feels lonely, he or she needs holding. Holding and soothing are important to help get over the "bumps" in life. "Bumps" can be hurt feelings as well as knees and elbows.

3. Provide opportunities for success. Not every child will grow and learn according to the charts in child development books. Every child is different. You know your child best. Follow his or her growth and progress patterns and plan learning experiences that he or she can handle. A child should not be forced to eat solid foods, to ride a bicycle, or to learn to read at an early age just because someone else's child does or because the chart says so. Teach and guide your child in new activities. Use training wheels and be there to hold the bike when you take them off. Assign tasks and guide your child to the successful completion of the task. A baby who takes down books from the shelf can find just as much fun in putting them back if it is a shared experience. Give praise while you work together. As the child gets older, putting the books back will be an easy task that can be assigned and only checked on. If you tell your five-year-old "Clean your room," he or she probably will not know where to start. If you break the cleaning into small tasks such as "Put all the books on the bookshelf" and "Put the dirty clothes in the hamper," the room eventually will be clean. If you give guidance and praise after each completed task, you are guiding and teaching your child how to approach the problem of the entire room. It is a successful experience.

From the first time you share in the fun of putting the stuffed animals to sleep in their box or the books on the shelf, until the time you can say, "If you want your allowance, the trash has to be emptied and your room straight," you are guiding your child to success. *You are asking for no more than your child is capable of doing, training him or her to do it, monitoring his or her attention to the task, and praising when the task is completed.*

From the time your child enters a mother's-day-out program until he or she graduates from high school, help him or her to feel successful. Parents can help with the little things. Make sure your child has the supplies needed. Make sure an item is ready for Show and Tell. If the children are learning about a topic that is of special interest to you or your child, help him or her to share items with the group. Take refreshments on special occasions. (He or she will probably get to serve.) Attend your child's activities as often as possible—from the first mother's-day-out open house to the high school science fair or basketball game. Help your child be successful by being involved.

Think and Talk About

Let this book be a model. Just as this book was written to relieve your doubts about your parenting skills by letting you know that most of what you are doing is right—and just as this book says it is okay to make some mistakes and praises you for caring about and seeking information on parenting skills—you will be doing the same for your child. You will help relieve your child's doubts by letting him or her know what he or she is doing right, and you will help and guide him or her with the things that are not going right. You will allow for some mistakes to be made along the way. And you will praise the child for any steps in the right direction. Success will come for the child through your patience and guidance.

4. Help your child express himself or herself. To feel good about himself or herself, a child must be able to communicate. To be able to express feelings and share ideas, a child must have early and continued practice with language. Do not feel uncomfortable or foolish talking to a baby. He or she may not talk back, but that is how language is learned. Talk, listen, and ask questions. Do not assume that exposure, even to educational television programs, can take the place of conversations you have with your child. Take every opportunity to expose your child to language. Talk during diapering about body parts and clothing. "Let's change your diaper. How about I put you on the bed to do it? I'm going to take the wet one off. Your bottom is so wet. If you hold your legs still, we'll finish sooner. Your skin is so smooth. Your diaper rash is better. We finished fast. Let's go to the kitchen and warm your bottle. I think you are hungry."

As the child begins to use words, show interest and talk about the objects he or she is using—you will be giving him or her the names of the objects. As the child starts to use sentences, talk about his or her requests or statements. When a child starts to express ideas, ask questions for further understanding and add to his or her ideas with additional information. Ask your child how he or she feels about things that happen, both good and bad.

77

Positive ways of expressing feelings are important to emotional health. Having to show anger because he or she has not learned to communicate it with words can cause trouble. Above all, listen and show interest. As the child grows older and problems arise, his or her willingness and ability to talk to you and others will help him or her reach out for solutions. If you want to be able to communicate with your teenager, you must begin the sharing of thoughts and feelings in the infant stage. Talk, listen, ask questions, stay interested, show understanding, and make suggestions!

5. Praise your child often. Praise has been mentioned many times in this book. Praising your child is so important to self-concept and well-being, however, that it deserves a section of its own. Praise your child for a job well done, when improvement is made, or when he or she tries hard. Waiting for perfection to give praise may keep your child from feeling successful. He or she will get an "I can" attitude by realizing that improvement or trying hard counts as much as success. You will be saying that with gradual improvement, you expect him or her to succeed. Your encouragement during difficult tasks is important.

Think and Talk About

There are many ways and words to use to say "great job!" to your child. Check out the following words of praise. Think about times you can use some of them to praise your child.

Positive/Esteem-Building Remarks	Negative/Accusatory Remarks & Remarks of Conditional Approval
"Tell me more about... [your coloring]." [this homework]."	"You [colored in the lines/did your homework] perfectly."
"You made a good effort...[when you tried to read that]." [to stay at day care for the whole day]."	"You're the best player on the team." "I'm sure the teacher likes you the best."
"I see you are excited about... [the party]." [visiting grandpa]."	"If you don't quiet down we're not going to the party."
"You've really learned that well."	"That's right, do it this way." "Try harder next time."
"I like the way you... [pay attention]." [have fun with the game]." [share with your sister]."	"Why can't you... [do what I tell you?]" [follow the rules?]"
"I don't like... [to see a big mess in your room]." [to hear back talk]."	"You made a mess of your room." "Don't [you] talk back to me."

Positive/Esteem-Building Remarks	Negative/Accusatory Remarks & Remarks of Conditional Approval
"Soon you'll be able to… [go to the potty]." [drink from a cup]."	"You're too little to do that."

Now it's your turn. Think of as many ways as you can of saying "good for you."

6. Share family problems. Talk to your child at his or her level about unusual family situations. Often a child senses a problem and then imagination makes it bigger than it is. When an angry parent or other member of the household leaves to cool off, the child may feel abandoned. If you leave in anger, take the child with you or arrange for someone to watch him or her. Always let your child know you will be back. Never leave for more than a few hours without making contact with your child or returning to pick him or her up. If you feel that you may take your anger out on the child or that your anger is caused by frustration over parenting, make a supervised contact. Take the child, along with another family member or friend, for a ride or walk. Make sure your child understands that it is the situation or behavior you do not like, not him or her.

If a family member or friend dies, explain the death at your child's level based on your religious training or beliefs. Never say that the person is asleep. If a child is told that death is sleep, he or she may become afraid to sleep for fear of never waking. In case of divorce or a decision to change your living situation because of a disagreement, make sure the child understands that it is not his or her fault. In most divorces, children tend to blame themselves, thinking "If only I had been better." Let your child know that separation or divorce is an adult problem and decision.

Keep family arguments as calm as possible. When you anticipate that a major event is going to cause an explosion from one parent or the other, you may want to arrange for your child to stay with friends or relatives temporarily. Normal discussions during a disagreement should be experienced by a child. He or she needs to know that anger and disappointment can be expressed reasonably. A child should also be allowed to see adult tears. Unhappiness and working to make things better are part of life. Yes, adults—both men and women—do cry and go on with life.

If a major change is occurring, the child needs to be prepared for it. As soon as you know that you will be moving, getting a divorce, changing your child's baby-sitter or day care, or adding a family member, start preparing your child. Let him or her know about the change and the reason for the change. Show understanding of the loss he or she feels. Share positive aspects of the change, such as having a park near your new home, being closer to your work, getting a better job, going back to school, or making new friends.

7. Dress your child appropriately. Your child's clothing should be comfortable, clean, and not too different from that of the average child. Parents often dress newborns for how the clothing looks instead of for comfort. If you are going on a special outing such as a family gathering, a religious service, or dinner in a restaurant, it is understandable that you will want to dress up your child. You can dress your baby for both comfort and looks, however. Select the fabric of the clothing carefully. It should not scratch or irritate the baby's skin. The child should not be too hot or cool. The clothing should fit properly. Dress the baby in everyday clothing for comfort as soon as the event is over, especially for the ride home. If plastic pants must be used, remove them as soon as possible and allow the baby to go without a diaper for a while when you arrive home. Change the baby's diaper at the gathering as often as you would at home. Comfort and prevention of irritation and rashes are important for the baby.

When you dress a baby or child for mother's-day-out, for day care, or for school, do not use your child's best clothing. Dress your child in play or school clothes. He or she will just be working and playing with friends. If you send the child off to play in a best outfit, do not blame him or her if it gets torn or stained. Let the child learn, work, and play without being overly concerned about the care of clothing. Accidents will happen!

Even school-age children need parental guidance on cleanliness and choosing clothing. Young children seldom notice when a child is dressed in ordinary play or school clothes, even hand-me-downs. Concern about style and purchase price comes later. However, even the youngest school-age groups will notice and avoid a child who is dirty or who wears clothes that are not clean. Remind your child to bathe in the morning if he or she wets the bed. Children who wet the bed and do not bathe often are frequently left out of group activities by other children. As a child gets older, he or she will often leave the group if cleanliness is a problem. Keep clean, appropriate clothes available for your child.

8. Teach your child to be thoughtful, courteous, and respectful. One the hardest questions to answer is "Why don't I have friends?" For some children it is only a temporary experience. It might happen occasionally when he or she is tired and has been disagreeable and grouchy. Or the available children are older and leave the younger child out of activities. For other children who have not been taught how to relate to other people, the loneliness may last through one of their developmental stages—or a lifetime. The old saying "You can't buy friendship" is true. Neither can parents make other children, even brothers and sisters, play with a child. Real friendship is earned. Getting along with others is important throughout life. People who get along with others have an advantage in school and jobs.

Your child will learn to relate to others from what he or she hears you say or do. You are your child's model for this lifelong skill. Your child learns from you to be thoughtful, respectful, and courteous to others. As a parent you model even when you do not realize it. The way to teach this skill is to be friendly, show you care about others, and talk with your child about why you are doing these things. If you model sharing, your child will learn to share. Praise your child when he or she shows kindness to or shares with other children or adults.

Think about what you would say to a child who asked how to make friends. Many educators have trouble answering this question for a child. If it is a problem of not relating to others, you are dealing with a very fragile child. Be careful. So many of the things parents might say at this point come out negative and full of blame. Some parents may even ignore the problem or say about the other child, "Who cares what he does?" or "Why do you care about her? Just stay at home." Removing a child from other children should be only temporary; it is not a solution. Begin to look at how you relate to others or talk about them when they walk away. Your child is watching and learning. A child who relates to others and enjoys being with both adults and other children will feel better about him- or herself.

Think and Talk About

Special Obstacles for Teen Parents in Building the Child's Self-Concept and Self-Confidence

⇨ ***A limited number of people are available to share the responsibility of parenting with the teen parent.*** A single parent who is parenting alone may feel overwhelmed. He or she may not be able to devote the amount of time needed to provide the child with support. Recognizing the need is the first step. Finding ways to build your child's self-concept and self-confidence while taking care of the routine is step two. Read this chapter again and make notes of simple everyday suggestions that you can carry out during routine child care.

➥ *Teen parents are in the adolescent stage of human growth and development.* Adolescence is a learning and growing time. It is a time of insecurity and instability. Moods often change the teen's feelings about him- or herself and the world from day to day. Teen parents still need to reach out to others, including parents, for nurturing and reassurance. If a teen parent is to give a supporting hand to build a baby's self-concept, he or she also must be willing to reach for support from parents or other adults.

➥ *Life plans change or must be postponed.* To feel good about yourself and to have a good self-concept, you may need to set goals for the future. Changes or postponements do not have to be forever. Use chapter sixteen to set new dates for reaching those goals. Make the necessary plans to meet the goals. You will feel better about yourself. Then you can help your child develop those same good feelings—"I can and I will!"

➥ *Family structure changes.* Most teen parents need some form of financial support, either from their families or welfare sources. Accepting help may make it difficult for the teen parent to feel independent, and the adolescent's belief in him- or herself may suffer. The good feelings that come from providing for a family may have to wait for later. Setting life goals to move toward financial independence is important. See chapter sixteen if your life goals have not been planned yet or need updating. Believe in your future as a provider; support from others can be temporary.

85

The Role of
Discipline

The busy parent's tone of voice shows displeasure as the infant tries to turn over during diapering. A one-year-old is scolded for accidentally knocking over a glass of milk at dinner. Diapering and spilt milk are just a part of day-to-day living with a baby. There are times when a child should not be scolded or punished. Rather, the guidance the child should receive is called *discipline*.

Discipline Is Not Punishment

Parents often talk about discipline as punishment. A parent might ask, "How do you discipline your child? By spanking?" Another might answer, "I discipline my child by sitting him in time-out for five minutes." They are talking about punishment. Punishment is the consequence of breaking a rule.

In contrast, *discipline means providing structure*. A child must be given boundaries. He or she must understand what can be done and where he or she is allowed to go. *Discipline is establishing rules, rewards, and consequences.* The child needs to know not only what is expected of him or her but also what will happen if a rule is broken and what can be expected if he or she behaves. *Discipline requires consistent, immediate, firm, and fair follow-through by the parent. It can be described as sure, fast, and just.*

The overall goal of discipline is for the child to learn self-control and then to take responsibility for his or her actions. This does not happen on its own. The parent is the teacher, model, and judge who constantly guides the child until adulthood. Your baby will be in training throughout childhood. As the baby grows older, his or her world expands to include other places and other people. A parent will not always be with the child to tell him or her what to do or when he or she is right or wrong. The child will have to behave according to the day-to-day training received in the past.

Motto for Discipline: It's Not the Child

Your little one must understand that it is the behavior you do not like, not the child. The love you give should be unconditional. That means that despite misbehavior you love and care for the child. It is not, "You make me so angry." It is, "Your behavior makes me angry."

Think about the above statements about discipline. What do they mean to you, the parent, in the day-to-day training of your child?

Provide Structure. Set Rules. Set limits to your child's world. A child feels safe and secure when he or she knows the boundaries. You are teaching and showing your child:

⇝ What will hurt (Is this safe?).

⇝ What can be broken easily (Should I be touching this?).

87

➷ The things that do not belong to him or her (Is this mine? Is this a toy?).

➷ His or her space (Can I open this cabinet? Am I allowed in this room?)

➷ What should be spoken (Is this a bad word? Am I hurting someone's feelings?).

If the limits are too loose, too strict, or inconsistent (enforced only some of the time), minor problems can turn into major ones. Parents sometimes make rules that are *too loose.* An extreme example of this is allowing a child to climb on a dangerous stair railing with no guidance from the parent other than "If you fall, it will be your own fault." Another example would be a parent setting boundaries by saying, "Stay where I can see you." What are the child's boundaries? A small child involved in play should not be expected to keep up with where the parent is. The limits must be specific: "Stay inside the fence. Do not open the gate."

Rules can also be *too strict.* A parent who makes a child stay on the porch even though there is a childproof fenced yard and adult supervision is being strict without reason. The parent who walks a child every step from the car to the classroom when the drop-off area is supervised is too protective. The parent is not using the safe, supervised situation to build the child's sense of responsibility. How can a child learn if not given a chance to try?

Parents often are guilty of enforcing rules *inconsistently.* When a parent is too tired, too busy, or is entertaining company, he or she may not follow through with enforcing rules. Sometimes a parent who is already upset may be too quick to react to a child's inappropriate behavior. One of the main reasons children continue to misbehave or to test limits is that sometimes they "get away with it." When a child continues to test your limits, he or she is saying "When is my parent going to do something?" The child isn't sure. Being consistent does not mean that you have to punish your child every time. However, the child must be stopped every time. He or she must be reminded of the rule, the reason for the rule, and the consequence of breaking it. If it happens again, following through with the consequence is a must. Warning too often becomes a meaningless threat.

Help the Child Understand What Is Expected. Parents must not only set standards and limits that "fit" the child's age but also help the child understand what is expected. One way parents help children understand is by modeling appropriate behavior. Parents set an example by behaving appropriately themselves. Another way to help children understand is to give reasons for the rules: "You can't go near the stove because you could get burned." With crawlers, parents just pick the baby up and put him or her back where he or she belongs. With a toddler, parents depend on the word "no" with an explanation and also remove the child from the situation. As a child grows older, parents can expect more understanding of the established rules. The child will know that if a rule is broken, the consequence will follow. The word "no" is not used as often. At this age and stage of growth, using "no" more than once is just threatening the child. Follow-through is important.

Think and Talk About

As you read the following examples of three different families' ways of handling inappropriate language, ask yourself these questions: Were the parents' expectations about bad language understood? Did the parents model the right behavior for the child? Were the parents consistent in their follow-through? Did the child deserve punishment?

Bob and Zelda's two-year-old son Jack repeated his father's favorite descriptive word when his toy car crashed into the garage. His parents laughed. Two hours later, when Jack's seventeen-year-old uncle arrived, Bob asked Jack to tell Uncle Lance what he had said earlier when his car crashed. Little Jack repeated the word several times as his uncle laughed. Three days later, Jack was at a birthday party given by Bob's boss for his daughter, Sophia. Sophia pulled a toy truck from Jack's hand. He called her his father's favorite descriptive world. Bob took Jack to the bathroom and spanked him.

Leshawn and Diane made a decision at the birth of their child, Georgia, to stop using inappropriate language around their home. They both enjoyed a joke and occasionally used certain words with friends to make a point. It didn't mean they changed totally, but it did mean that they didn't use off-color language in the presence of their child. As the models of "good" and "bad" language for their child, they had set the expectations. When Georgia called her dog a @#$%&, Leshawn and Diane knew she had not heard it from *them. As they explained to Georgia why she should not use such words, they could say "Mommy and Daddy do not use those words."*

Angel and Anna enjoyed telling jokes and using "bad" language to make a point with each other and friends. When their twins, Roberto and Angelina, called each other these same words while playing ball, the parents explained to their children that only adults could use those words and only in certain places.

Communicate Reasons. As a child is removed, told "no," or given a new rule, the child should be told why. This is very important to future behavior when the child must make decisions. A child will move toward self-control sooner if he or she understands the reasons for not doing certain things. He or she knows: "Grandma has worked hard on this. It isn't mine. I must leave it alone" or "Needles aren't safe. I could hurt myself or someone else."

Occasionally a parent sets strict limits or gives a harsh consequence just because "I said so." The parent is not being just and fair. The child's understanding and trust in the parent's guidance are at stake. On the other hand, a child may need to be removed from danger quickly. The parents will have to make a new rule fast. They may have to raise their voices to show urgency. The child may have climbed a high railing or have a bottle of medication open. To keep the child safe, a command can be given quickly without explanation, then explained later.

Establish Consequences. Like rules, consequences must be set and never changed in anger. The punishment must not be too harsh or last too long. If the consequence is too harsh you may cause emotional or physical harm to your child. If it is too long and interferes with family activities, you will find yourself not following through with it. If you do not follow through, the child will be misled into thinking that it is okay to behave inappropriately. Or you may become frustrated and angry if the behavior continues. You may punish the child too harshly.

The consequences should "fit the crime" *and* "fit the child." Spanking a crying infant is not appropriate. It does not "fit the child" and there is no "crime." Taking away a child's toys for a week because he or she knocked over a flowerpot does not "fit the crime." Making the child help to clean it up or using his or her allowance to replace it is appropriate. If you use time-out, limit the time to ten to fifteen minutes. When a child receives a shorter period, he or she will tend to serve it gracefully and still feel punished. Use a timer: The time seems to tick on forever. Do not allow begging or whining to win reprieve, but do give a few minutes off for good behavior in time-out.

Spanking (inflicting physical pain) should be used as a last resort. It is a harsh consequence for the breaking of a minor rule or a rule that does not involve safety. If you spank, do so only under the following conditions: (1) never as an overreaction to your anger; (2) only if spanking has been established as a possible consequence; (3) only if the child has memory and is at least two years old and no more than ten; and (4) no more than three reasonable "swats" are given, only on the child's bottom. (Even minor marks on the child or slapping or hitting anywhere other than the child's bottom should be considered abuse. See chapter twelve for more information.)

Parents who enforce rules and give consequences inconsistently are misleading their child. The rule is to stay inside the yard, but the parent brags the first time the child unlatches the gate or climbs over the fence. The parent might go so far as to have the child perform the "new trick" for others. The child may assume that it is okay some of the time and maybe even "cute." Imagine the child's surprise at being punished the next time he or she leaves the yard. Rules must be enforced consistently for a child to follow them consistently.

Think and Talk About

A young mother and the uncle of a nineteen-month-old girl were attempting to teach the child not to touch her uncle's cigarettes. "Go ahead and touch the cigarettes," they said to the eager and curious child. But each time she touched them, the mother or uncle spanked her. She began to cry in frustration. Not only was the child being misled by being told to touch the cigarettes, she also was being punished for doing as she was told. The child was not given clear signals. Did the child understand what the adults expected? Was the child breaking a rule?

Establish routines.

Two-and-a-half-year-old Sebastian knows that either his dad or his mom will pick him up this afternoon at his friend Toby's house. Sometimes Toby's mom will pick the boys up from nursery school and watch them until one of Sebastian's parents can get him after work. But then Sebastian is never sure whether he will go home to rest, eat dinner at a fast-food restaurant, or get dropped off at his grandparents' house. Sometimes it feels like forever until he gets home. When he is hungry and tired he is in a bad mood. Today Toby's mom didn't have any snacks except for some root beer, and Sebastian is hungry. When Sebastian's mom finally picks him up, he starts to cry and runs away from her. She yells, "Come here right now! We have to go to the store to get food!" but he will not listen. Embarrassed in front of Toby's mom, she grabs her son and drags him, kicking and screaming, to the car outside. But Sebastian thinks, "I just want to know where I'm going next and when I'll get to eat and rest. That would make it easier for me to behave!"

Follow Through Firmly, Fairly, and Consistently. You will be telling your child that you love and care about him or her. You will be fostering your child's respect for you and helping him or her feel secure. You do not leave your child guessing about who is in charge.

Think and Talk About

Are You Firm? Do you follow through immediately each time an established rule is broken? Do you repeatedly threaten? Does "no" always mean "no"?

More Discipline (Fair)

Juanita often visits her parents' home with her eighteen-month-old toddler, Leena, who loves to crawl

94

and walk around the large house. Even though Leena is often there, Juanita's parents enjoy keeping their house furnished with expensive and ornate decorations. Many are precious pieces of folk art from Ecuador. One day, while her mother's back is turned for only a minute, little Leena climbs on to the couch and tries to grasp a glass lamp on a nearby table. Just before the lamp topples over and crashes to the floor, Juanita turns around and, in one quick movement, rights the lamp. Then she picks Leena up and places her on the floor. "No, Leena, we do not touch grandma's things. They are very special to her." Although Juanita's first impulse is to spank the child, she does not do so as she realizes that Leena was only exploring and could not have known how breakable the lamp is. Instead, she takes her baby to another room and plays hide-and-seek with her. "Next time we visit," Juanita thinks, "I will have to plan some activities to keep Leena busy and bring plenty of toys along, too."

Are You Fair? Do you change the rules or increase the consequences when you are angry? Do you go overboard on consequences? Have you prepared for each stage of growth your child will go through? Remember, a crawler can find new places, a walker can go faster, and climbers can reach higher. As your child develops new interests, do you expand the boundaries? If a child learns to use bubble soap to blow bubbles, he or she will have to be allowed outside. When a child gets a bike, he or she needs to be able to use the sidewalk.

Are You Consistent? Do you follow through each time a rule is broken? Do you allow having visitors, being in a public place, or being tired to keep you from following through? Do you give small jobs, teach, help, and praise as the child works? Do you make sure the task is complete? Do you laugh or smile about the use of bad words and inappropriate actions at home, then expect your child not to use them outside the home?

Plan Ahead for Problems. A child's life should be as trouble-free as possible. If your child and a neighbor child can't play without fighting, do not allow them to play unsupervised. If Aunt Jane's house is full of glass objects, plan your trips without the child or ask that the items be removed. Take plenty of toys for your child. How about a playpen? If grocery shopping is a problem, take a trip with the child when you do not need to shop. Retrain your child: "You will ride in the basket. You will not reach for the shelves. We will buy only the items on our list."

Turn Discipline Time into Learning Time. As you enforce rules, give a positive alternative—a "fun choice." For example, say, "That's grandma's needlepoint. She has worked hard on it and we don't want to damage her work. You could hurt yourself on the needle. Let's find some old magazines in the box grandma made for you. Have you ever cut out paper dolls? Let's make a family." Another example: "Those are Aunt Wanda's dolls and they must stay on the shelf. They are not the kind for play. Let's find your doll and make a bed out of this box." By giving your child something different to do, you have removed him or her from the trouble spot. You have given a choice. By involving the child in another fun activity, you've turned trouble time into fun time.

Attention Deficit Hyperactivity Disorder (ADHD)

According to the National Institute of Health Statistics, Attention Deficit Hyperactivity Disorder, or ADHD, affects five million children in the United States. If after you've tried the methods of discipline outlined in this chapter, your child still has trouble focusing attention, controlling hyperactivity, and shows no thought (appropriate for his or her age) before acting, seek medical help. Doctors can assess the situation and, if necessary, prescribe drugs, recommend expert help, and educate you. If your child is diagnosed with ADHD, also known as ADD (Attention Deficit Disorder), you will have to be especially careful to use brief and clear directions that are not yelled or repeated more than twice. Maintain a definite schedule and very consistent rules.

Parents Teach and Model Responsibility

Children learn responsible behavior from their parents. You are modeling responsibility all the time. Children imitate you even when you do not want them to do so. What are you modeling for your child? Are you going to work or school on time? Do you stay home only when ill? Are you meeting your family's needs? Do you handle money and billpaying promptly and carefully? Do food purchases come before entertainment? Is your baby/child clean and comfortable? Do you finish your household chores?

Suggestions for Teaching Responsibility:

1. Plan together and assign reasonable, valuable chores for all family members. As the child grows older, set daily age-appropriate jobs. The tasks should be something your child can do. Break the jobs into small chunks. A task such as "Clean your room" can be broken into several separate ones: "Pick up your toys." "Put your clothes in the hamper." "Put your books on the shelf." Teach your child to do the job and monitor him or her until the task is complete. Praise your child after each chunk of the job is completed.

2. Guide and model the need, method, and schedule for bathing, brushing of teeth, hair combing, and wearing of clean, appropriate clothes. Allow your child to learn and earn control of grooming and clothing, but monitor before he or she leaves the house each time.

3. Make mealtime a family gathering time. It is not a time for television or telephone calls. It is a time for parents to teach and guide appropriate manners for eating and for children to practice them. In case of spills by a small child, share the responsibility of clean-up and teach how. When the child is capable, have a small bucket of water and sponge ready and give him or her the responsibility. (Children starting preschool are definitely ready to take charge). The family will have time for conversation and sharing for all members.

Respect for each other and each other's opinions can be modeled.

4. Model the importance of good nutrition and fitness. Have family members take responsibility for having healthy bodies. Plan meals together that include all the food groups. Eliminate junk foods, including sugar-coated cereals. Limit snacks to foods like nuts, fresh fruits and vegetables, low-fat milk, cheese, beef jerky, peanut butter, popcorn, unsweetened juices, raisins and other dried fruits, whole wheat crackers and bread, pickles, and granola. Plan family activities that require physical exercise and schedule outside play for children. Good eating habits and sufficient activity lead to good health and decrease weight problems.

5. Model and teach the care of personal items. Require and guide children to put away and take care of toys and clothing. A toy that is deliberately broken or neglected should not be replaced. More toys should not be purchased until the child takes responsibility for the ones he or she already has.

6. Teach responsibility by having your child share in the care of any pets the family has. To prevent an animal from suffering as your child takes over the responsibility, monitor the care. (A child should not be responsible for a pet until he or she is ready and capable.)

7. Use an allowance to teach money management. (Read a guide on allowances before you start.)

Think and Talk About

Special Obstacles for Teen Parents in Building the Child's Self-Concept and Self-Confidence

➩ *Teen parents are in the adolescent stage of human growth and development.* Teens are still in training for adulthood and may still require structure and guidance. The adolescent is just beginning to take responsibility for his or her own care, support, and behavior. At the same time the teen parent is required to begin supporting and training a child. One of the problems that all parents face is that they are familiar with only one type of discipline, the type used by their own parents. Teens who live at home are still receiving that discipline. To understand other ways of handling a situation, teens will have to read about them or observe other parents in action. Reread this chapter when you find that your child is out of control or you find yourself just yelling.

Teens who have been abused or who are currently being abused may become abusers of their children. If this sounds familiar, get help early—for yourself *and* your child. Discipline should not be punishment.

➩ *Family structure changes.* Three-generation living creates some discipline problems. Who should the child listen to—the parent or the grandparent? The adults must agree on a plan for discipline. Give your parents reasons for changing the structure in the household. Too many orders and frequent changing of the rules and consequences will only confuse the child.

Staying Healthy

Well Baby Appointments and Preventive Care

Many children are growing up healthier and living longer as adults because of the preventive care given to them throughout life. Your doctor or clinic will make recommendations about how often your baby or child needs checkups. For the child who is not doing well, regular visits help the doctor detect the problems early. For a child who is developing normally, the visits help reassure the new parent and guide him or her through basic child care. With the first baby, you may have more questions and may need more frequent advice. Be sure to take your child for regular visits. (If you want more frequent visits, ask for them.) As the baby gets older, the appointments are less frequent, but they are still important.

During each appointment, the doctor examines the baby and advises you of any special needs. The baby is weighed and measured. Physical and mental development are checked. Immunizations (shots) are given. The visits are also a time to tell the doctor about your baby's development. When did baby cut the first tooth? Is he or she crawling now? You also have time to ask questions. Do not be bashful. No question is too simple or too foolish to ask if you do not know the answer. Have a list ready; you might forget to ask about something you need to know. Do not count on the doctor to have printed information on the questions you ask; have pen and paper ready to take notes. You may need to write down when and in what order to start your baby on solid foods. You may have to write down the name of an over-the-counter vitamin or medication if you are not familiar with it. (Your notes from the doctor added to your notes of baby's growth and development will be good records and fun memories for you and your child when he or she is grown.)

Do not leave the office with any doubts. If you get home and need more information or are not sure about the doctor's instructions, do not hesitate to call back. Often the nurse can clarify the doctor's orders. If not, he or she is only a few steps away from the doctor and the answers. Nurses are also available to help with basic childcare questions when you cannot reach the doctor. Do not hesitate to call the doctor or nurse between visits. Your baby's health and well-being may be at stake.

Choosing a Doctor

You can check with family, friends, or neighbors for recommendations for a pediatrician or general practitioner for your baby. If your health insurance plan only covers certain doctors, you will save a lot of money by seeing one of them. Try to get recommendations for a doctor accepted by your plan. If that is not possible, interview the doctor yourself. Firsthand information is the best.

When shopping for merchandise, you look for quality, price, and compatibility with you and your interests. Do the same when "shopping" for a doctor. If possible, make an appointment with the doctor at least two weeks before your baby is due. Interview the doctor to make sure he or she is qualified and is available when needed. If the doctor is not covered by your insurance plan, make sure that you can afford the fees and a payment plan. Also check out the office. Is there room to wait with your infant? Does the doctor provide separate waiting areas for well and sick patients? Does the doctor have a private or a group practice? Who will cover for him or her if it is a private practice? In a group practice, will your baby see his or her doctor most often? Consider travel time to the office and the doctor's hospital. Prepare for baby's first two weeks by asking about the newborn exam, breast-feeding or formula, vitamins, circumcision, and medications to keep on hand. Make sure you know the doctor's emergency policy and after-hours number.

Illness

Knowing When Your Child Is Ill

Your baby is usually happy and pleasant. But today he or she is irritable, fussy, or crying, or has become listless. There seems to be no reason for the change in behavior. He or she just does not feel well.

Look for these *other signs of illness.* Call the doctor immediately regardless of the hour for those listed in boldface type below:

⮑ Appetite loss

⮑ **Bleeding** that cannot be stopped with pressure.

- **Breathing problems** that are severe: blue lips, enlarged nostrils, struggling for breath, unable to make any noise though conscious.

- Color change: flushed or pale.

- **Cough** that is severe: loud, deep, and dry with fever above 102°F.

- **Diarrhea** that is severe: unusual thirst, dry mouth, no wet diapers in six hours (less than six if child is under two months); hard to wake (if child is under two months, listless); sunken eyes; blood-tinged bowel movement, abdominal pain or rumbling tummy.

- **Drowsiness** or fitful sleep.

- **Earache** with a stiff neck and rectal temperature of 102°F.

- **Eyes** that are swollen, red, and itchy or painful.

- **Fever** above 103°F taken rectally.

- **Headache** that persists more than twelve hours.

- **Unusual sweating**.

- **Urine** reduced or blood tinged.

- **Vomiting** repeatedly, plus temperature above 102°F or presence of blood in vomit.

- Watery, glassy, red, or sensitive eyes.

Calling the Doctor

Knowing when to call a doctor comes from experience. If you are in doubt, call the doctor's office or the clinic for advice. Call as soon as the infant shows signs of illness. Keep the doctor informed. A trip to the doctor's office may be necessary. The doctor may need to see the baby to diagnose the illness. Many times a shot is necessary to stop the illness, or the doctor may need to take a throat culture or urine specimen. The doctor has the necessary equipment in his office. Be prepared to take the baby or child there.

In an Emergency . . .

The following form is designed for use in advance of an emergency. You can use notebook paper or a copy machine at the library. *Have a pencil ready to record the doctor's instructions.*

Temperature: _____

Doctor's Emergency Number: _____

Skin Color: _____

Attitude and Behavior of Infant: _____

Length of Time Showing Symptoms: _____

    ➭ Listlessness _____

    ➭ Irritability _____

    ➭ Cough _____

    ➭ Runny nose _____

⮑ Ear pulling _____

_____

⮑ Abnormal bowel movements _____

⮑ Other _____

⮑ Medications given (how much and when?)
   Acetaminophen (Tylenol)_____
   Decongestant _____
   Cough syrup _____

Regional Poison Control Number _____
Drugstore Hours and Number_____
Twenty-four-hour Drugstore and Number_____
Doctor's Instructions:_____

_____

_____

_____

_____

Think and Talk About

The decision to call your baby's doctor may be based on symptoms, your instinct, or your need for reassurance that the baby is all right. List two times that you should call the doctor and two times that calling your mother or a friend is the best choice.

Taking a Baby's Temperature
Fever is a symptom of illness that shows the body's

attempt to fight it off. Practice taking baby's temperature before he or she becomes ill. Knowing what to do will keep you calm when your baby is sick. For children under the age of two, take the child's temperature using a rectal thermometer; the end is rounded instead of pointed. (Digital thermometers and instant ear thermometers generally are used for children two and older.) Follow these steps:

1. Firmly hold the end of the thermometer opposite the bulb (it will break if hit or dropped).

2. Shake vigorously until the reading is below 96°F.

3. Dip the bulb in petroleum jelly (Vaseline).

4. Place baby face down on a diaper over your lap, with legs hanging down.

5. Insert the bulb about an inch into the rectum by gently allowing it to find its own direction. Do not force.

6. Hold the thermometer in place between two fingers with your hand flat against baby's bottom. Do not let go. Wait three minutes.

7. Remove the thermometer and place the baby in a safe place.

8. Read the thermometer: hold it horizontally away from light and roll it until you can see the mercury line and the numbers. The degrees are numbered, and each mark is a fifth of a degree. On a

rectal thermometer, normal body temperature is 99.6°F.

9. Clean the thermometer with soap and water, return it to its case, and put it away in a safe place.

Treating a Baby with a Fever

Keep the room no warmer than 68° or 70°F and dress the baby lightly. Give him or her plenty of liquids and a fever-reducing medication if recommended by your doctor. Use a lukewarm tub or sponge bath to bring the fever down. This lowers the baby's body temperature.

Giving Medication

Above all, follow the doctor's orders. If medication is ordered, be sure to give it according to directions. Administer the entire prescription even if the child gets better, unless the doctor orders otherwise. If your child attends day care or school, bring the medication in its original container along with any other information requested. Do not interrupt the giving of medication just because the child will not be with you. To be sure that you give the correct dosage, you need a dropper or syringe that is calibrated for measurement.

Do:

1. Keep your face calm. Never let the baby know that you think the medicine tastes nasty.

2. Hold the baby in a sitting position to prevent choking.

3. Place the dropper or syringe between the cheek and upper gum; slowly squeeze the dropper until empty.

4. Hold baby's lips shut until he or she swallows. If baby refuses to swallow, blow gently in his or her face.

Warning: Under no circumstances should anyone under age eighteen—either your child or you—take adult aspirin as a pain reliever or fever reducer or for any other reason. (Baby aspirin is fine.) The use of real aspirin by people under the age of eighteen has been linked to Reye's syndrome, a liver and brain disease.

Don't:

1. Use old prescriptions or one prescribed for another child

2. Mix medication with formula or juice, because the baby may not drink all of it

3. Say that medicine is candy

Baby's Own Medicine Cabinet

The items needed for baby care during illnesses are expensive. You may want to add them to your shower gift list or buy them one at a time. All items that belong to the baby should be kept in a safe and separate place.

- Absorbent cotton balls
- Antibiotic ointment

↪ Blunt scissors for trimming nails

↪ Decongestant recommended by doctor

↪ Fever-reducing medication, such as Infant Tylenol

↪ Hot-water bottle

↪ Measuring dropper or syringe

↪ Nose drops and syringe

↪ Ointment such as Desitin or A&D ointment for diaper rash

↪ Petroleum jelly

↪ Rectal thermometer

↪ Rubber bulb syringe for nose

↪ Rubbing alcohol and hydrogen peroxide

↪ Syrup of ipecac for inducing vomiting in case of poisoning. (Note: Use only when ordered by doctor or Poison Control Center.)

Home Care for Common Problems

Bruise. A bruise results from a trauma. Blood vessels under the skin are broken and internal bleeding occurs. Apply a cold compress or ice bag to the area for twenty minutes.

Burns. Apply cold (not ice) water immediately to lessen the pain and cleanse the wound. Bandage minor burns with sterile gauze. Burns often need medical attention. Call your doctor for any burn on a baby's hands, face, or genitals that produces blisters or raw spots or that becomes infected.

Circumcision Care. Rinse the penis at each diaper change with water from a cotton ball and apply petroleum jelly or an antibiotic ointment for three or four days. Consult your doctor if there is fresh blood or redness and swelling.

Common Colds. A cold is an upper-respiratory (nasal cavity and throat) infection. Ear or sinus infection, bronchitis, and pneumonia can complicate the illness. It is important that the baby is made comfortable and given plenty of clear liquids and less milk unless you are breast-feeding. In one of your first doctor visits with your baby, ask about over-the-counter medications as well as herbal remedies such as echinacea that may help relieve symptoms.

Constipation. If the baby's stool is hard, dry, or difficult to pass, try giving additional fluids, adding one tablespoon of prune juice to one bottle a day, or giving fruits or vegetables to a baby who is already eating solid food. Call the doctor if the stool is hard to pass or contains blood, if the baby is also vomiting, or if he or she becomes pale, listless, or irritable. Do not give a laxative or an enema unless the doctor orders it.

Convulsions. Convulsions are recognized by a sudden jerking movement of the body. They are caused by an irritation to the brain and often occur at the beginning of a cold or the flu. Having them in infancy does not mean they will recur in childhood or adulthood. To avoid injury to the baby, use gentle restraint. Check the baby's breathing and color. Roll him or her to the side if there is vomiting. During a convulsion, do not put anything in the baby's mouth nor give medications. Convulsions are not minor, so call your doctor immediately. If the convulsion was caused by fever, bring the fever down (see earlier in this chapter).

Cuts. A cut may be a minor scratch or a deep wound. The first thing to do for both is to stop the bleeding. A scratch should then be washed with soap and water, cleaned with hydrogen peroxide, and watched for signs of infection. A deeper wound may require a doctor's care if the bleeding does not stop or stitches are needed. The doctor will decide whether a tetanus booster shot is necessary.

Diaper Rash. This skin irritation begins as a reddish coloration. It is caused by allowing the baby to remain wet or in prolonged contact with its bowel movement. To care for diaper rash, leave the baby's bottom uncovered each day as long as possible and stop the use of rubber pants temporarily. After bowel movements, remove the diaper immediately and clean the area with something soft. Dip the baby's bottom in water occasionally during diaper changes and apply Desitin or A&D ointment or another ointment approved by your doctor. Watch for and report to your doctor any blisters or long-lasting rashes, which may signal a yeast infection.

Diarrhea. Frequent loose and watery stools often are caused by an infection from a virus, bacterium, or other germ. Less common causes are allergies, malabsorption of food, or immune deficiencies. Diarrhea often accompanies high fever and forceful vomiting. The stool is green or yellow and may contain blood or mucus. The number of bowel movements is increased from the normal pattern of one or two in a bottle-fed infant and six or eight in a breast-fed infant.

Treatment includes taking the baby off formula and solids for twenty-four to forty-eight hours and giving only clear liquids. Babies under six months need sugar electrolyte products such as Lytren to replace sugar and minerals. Cut back on solids and do not introduce new juices. Feed a variety of natural juices, water, very weak tea, broth, Jello water with double the water, and flat soda at room temperature. If the baby is not vomiting, offer as much liquid as he or she wants. Breast-feeding babies may continue to nurse (if the milk is tolerated) to prevent a supply loss in your milk. When the baby is well, gradually return to solids, beginning with applesauce, bananas, carrots, rice cereal, and toast. He or she may return to formula within three to seven days. Watch for signs of dehydration such as decreased urination, mild lethargy, sticky saliva, dry mouth, or lack of tears. *Go to the emergency room immediately* if: the baby has sunken eyes or is listless; there is no improvement in twenty-four hours; there is blood in the stool; or the rectal temperature is 101°F or higher in a baby under three months. Prevent a relapse by washing your hands and fresh foods, refrigerating foods, and never giving the baby any food containing raw egg.

Earaches. Often accompanying a cold, earache can be prevented by using a bulb syringe to clear the nasal passages. You can tell that a baby has an earache if he or she pulls at one or both ears, loses appetite, has a fever, or is nauseated or vomits. See the doctor as soon as you suspect one is coming. Consider it an emergency if the baby's rectal temperature is 103°F or if he or she is hard to wake, has a stiff neck, or has a discharge of pus from the ears. Temporary hearing loss may occur with an infection, which can affect language development. In the case of recurring infections, which may cause permanent loss of hearing, doctors often recommend minor surgery.

Hiccups occur regularly after meals. They require no treatment. Sometimes drinking warm water will stop them.

Impetigo. A skin infection usually occurring on the face, hands, and arms, impetigo spreads easily. It is caused by the same organism as strep throat. The doctor will probably prescribe an antibiotic.

Nosebleeds are usually caused by dryness of the nasal passage and consequent picking at the nose, a trauma to the nose, or an upper-respiratory infection. They also can indicate high blood pressure. Pinch the nostrils closed and apply pressure while the baby leans forward. Estimate the amount of blood lost. Report to the doctor if repeated nosebleeds occur or if there is also unexplained bruising.

Poisoning. Prevent poisoning by keeping dangerous items out of the child's reach. Knowing what is poisonous or toxic is the first step. Some things are obvious: medications, gasoline, antifreeze, and cleaning fluids. Add talcum powder to your toxic list; if inhaled, it can cause coughing, wheezing, vomiting, and labored breathing. Add vitamins, nicotine, salt, nutmeg, mouthwash, and many household plants as well. If your baby or child inhales or drinks something toxic, call your doctor or the Poison Control Center. Keep syrup of ipecac available at all times, but give only when directed.

Teething. Most babies become cross and fretful and lose their appetite when teething. Let the baby chew on things, including his or her own fist. To relieve teething discomfort, massage the gums and provide teething rings or wet washcloths chilled in the refrigerator. Take care if you use Popsicles or ice cubes; babies can choke on them. Use Infants' Tylenol at bedtime only if directed by your doctor. Do not use a numbing ointment. CAUTION: Do not allow baby to chew on painted surfaces; they may contain lead-based paint.

Umbilical Cord. The cord will dry up and fall off within ten to fourteen days. If your doctor recommends that you clean it, gently wipe it with alcohol on a cotton ball and turn down the diaper to keep it dry. Notify the doctor if redness or drainage appears.

Urinary Infection. The symptoms are vague; they may include loss of appetite, vomiting, diarrhea, fever, and fussiness. By the time foul-smelling urine or slowed growth is noticed, there may be a chronic infection of the bladder or kidneys or both. If the infection goes untreated, the kidneys can be permanently damaged. Call the doctor immediately. To prevent infection, make sure that your baby is urinating regularly and do not allow bubble baths. Be sure girls wipe themselves from front to back.

Vomiting can be caused by a number of infections as well as by food allergies and noninfectious blockage. Watch for dehydration by being sure baby is urinating at least every six hours. At frequent intervals feed small amounts of clear liquids such as Lytren, a mixture of sugar and electrolytes. Give clear juices, flat soda, and Jello water. Do not give milk.

Prevention of Illness
Many childhood illnesses can be prevented or kept from spreading. Parents must teach and model for children the importance of:

- bathing

- washing hands before meals and after bathroom use

- keeping fingernails clean

- covering their mouths when coughing or sneezing

Emergency Care

Children often get sick or have accidents at times other than during the doctor's office hours. Sometimes the child is so ill or the accident so obviously serious that you must seek immediate help. Be prepared. Keep a list of emergency numbers by your telephone. List your doctor's number and the number of the nearest hospital or minor emergency center. When calling for help, be prepared to give your address, clear directions to your home, and your phone number. If you do not have a telephone, keep your list of emergency numbers handy and know where the nearest telephone is. If it is a pay phone, keep coins taped to your list. If it is at a neighbor's house, talk with the neighbor about emergency telephone use as soon as you move in. Learn to dislodge small objects from the throat. Even better, take a class in CPR (cardiopulmonary resuscitation) or first-aid.

Removing Objects from a Child's Throat
Babies and small children often choke on bites of food too large for them to swallow, small objects, and hard candies. Most problems can be prevented by keeping small objects out of the child's environment. However, precautions do not always prevent choking.

If your child chokes and stops breathing:

1. Lay the baby face down over your arm, with the head lower than the chest.

2. Support the child's head with your hand around his or her jaw and under the chest.

3. Rest your arm on your thigh.

117

4. With the heel of your other hand, give four rapid blows between the shoulder blades.

If the foreign object is not dislodged:

5. Turn the baby over by placing your free hand on the back and holding him or her between your hands and arms. Support the baby's chest, neck, and jaw with one hand and the back of the neck and head with the other hand. When you have the baby between your arms and hands, turn him or her face up.

6. Rest your arm on your thigh so that the baby's head is lower than the chest.

7. With your fingertips, push four times on the chest between the nipples. Hold your hand so that your fingertips run up and down the breastbone, not across it.

8. Repeat the procedure until the item is dislodged.

If the baby is unconscious after the object is dislodged, call 911 or the emergency number in your area for medical assistance.

1. While waiting for help, place the baby on his or her back, straddling your arm.

2. Tip the head back slightly.

3. Open your mouth wide and place it over the child's mouth and nose.

4. Give four quick, gentle puffs. Remove your mouth from the baby to breathe, but do not pause between puffs. (A puff is the amount of air you can hold in your cheeks.)

5. If the chest does not rise, turn the baby over and give four back blows. Turn again and give four chest thrusts.

Immunizations

All children should receive immunizations as scheduled by their doctor or clinic. Most of us have never seen the effects of such diseases as polio, measles, mumps, or whooping cough because immunization has become routine. The shots are begun at two months and follow a schedule. Unless the child is ill, the schedule must be followed. You usually are given a form called a "shot record" with the first immunizations. This becomes your child's permanent record and each additional shot is recorded on it. Keep the record in a safe place. You will need it if you move, change doctors or clinics, or enter your child in day care or school. Doctors and clinics will send records; however, you need to know where and when each shot was given.

Keeping a Health Record

The following form should be kept current for each child.

NAME_____ BIRTH DATE _____
BLOOD TYPE _____

Growth Record

Birth	Weight	Height
One Month	_____	_____
Two Months	_____	_____
Three Months	_____	_____
Four Months	_____	_____
Five Months	_____	_____
Six Months	_____	_____
Seven Months	_____	_____
Eight Months	_____	_____
Nine Months	_____	_____
Ten Months	_____	_____
Eleven Months	_____	_____
One Year	_____	_____
1 1/2 Years	_____	_____
Two Years	_____	_____
2 1/2 Years	_____	_____
Three Years	_____	_____
Four Years	_____	_____
Five Years	_____	_____
Six Years	_____	_____

Pregnancy/Childbirth Problems and Type of Delivery:

Immunization Schedule

Age	Vaccine	Data Given	Age Recommended
2 months	1st DPT and 1st Polio		
4 months	2nd DPT and 2nd Polio		
6 months	3rd DPT and 3rd Polio		

15 months   MMR
18 months   4th DPT and 4th Polio
4–6 years   5th DPT and 5th Polio
14–16 years Tetanus-Diphtheria

Test Results:
(A test for tuberculosis is given at twelve months and repeated at one- to two-year intervals.)

Illnesses/Injuries:

Medications/Reactions:

Allergies:

Dental Information:

Tooth	Temporary Teeth Should Appear (Month)	Date First Seen	Age (Month)	Care/Loss
Right Side (Upper)				
Central Incisor	7th–9th			
Lateral Incisor	8th–10th			
Cuspid	16th–18th			
First Molar	13th–14th			
Second Molar	20th–24th			
Left Side (Upper)				
Central Incisor	7th–9th			
Lateral Incisor	8th–10th			
Cuspid	16th–18th			

First Molar   13th–14th
Second Molar   20th–24th

Right Side (Lower)
Central Incisor   7th–9th
Lateral Incisor   8th–10th
Cuspid   16th–18th
First Molar   13th–14th
Second Molar   20th–24th

Left Side (Lower)
Central Incisor   7th–9th
Lateral Incisor   8th–10th
Cuspid   16th–18th
First Molar   13th–14th
Second Molar   20th–24th

Family Health History: (Document medical problems of parents, grandparents, and other relatives on both sides of the family. Information may be important in medical diagnosis for you, your child, or future generations.)

Eating Right

Good nutrition is important at every age and stage of life. It is especially important for women in the childbearing years, pregnant women, mothers who are breast-feeding, children, and adolescents. Good nutrition means eating enough of the right foods. Humans must have an adequate and balanced diet. Good nutrition is important not only to growth and development but also to prevention of disease and recovery from illness.

Poor nutrition is not just a problem of low-income people. Money is not the main factor. Junk foods are frequently more expensive than nutritious foods. For example, an apple or a banana often costs less than a candy bar. The problem is the food choices people make. Though wrong foods are a problem, overconsumption and imbalance of foods are issues as well. To have a healthy, energetic body, you must supply it with the right amount of the right fuel—the right foods.

Nutritional Needs of Girls and Women

A woman's total life nutrition can have a impact on her reproductive performance and health. Females should have a nutritious diet as children and adolescents. Women in the childbearing years, pregnant women, and breast-feeding mothers need nutrition care long before pregnancy. The changes and pressures of pregnancy make it difficult to alter old eating habits. A woman who is undernourished or who fails to gain weight during pregnancy is at a greater risk of having a low-birth-weight baby, who in turn is more likely to suffer physical and mental handicapping conditions. The risk is increased by the mother's use of alcohol or drugs or if she diets or smokes. Poor dietary habits and low weight gain of the mother increase the mortality rates for infants—that is, they decrease the chances of survival at birth. A life-long nutritious diet is the key to health for mother and baby. Immediate consultation with a doctor when pregnancy begins is also vital. Follow the diet the doctor suggests. If vitamins are prescribed, take them.

Mothers who breast-feed have an increased need for calories, protein, and certain minerals and vitamins. Your doctor can advise you. Not following his or her advice can endanger the mother's health. If eating habits are severely restricted, the infant's nutrition will be put at risk because of a decrease in milk production.

Nutritional Needs of Infants

Babies are nutritionally more vulnerable than humans of any other age group. Because of their fast growth and development, babies require foods high in nutrients. Babies with low birth weight, birth defects, or other problems may have special nutritional needs. Making up for low birth weight early is important. An inadequate diet or excesses or imbalances in feeding can cause permanent problems. In addition to providing nutrition, simply holding your baby during feeding builds a sense of trust in you and the new world. The first decision you must make is in the first stage of baby's life: feeding.

Milk-Feeding Stage—Birth to Four Months
Breast or Bottle?
The decision is usually a personal one made with the support of your partner. You can choose breast-feeding unless you have had breast reduction surgery; you have an illness or infection; you need a prescription drug that would be harmful to the baby; you must be away from baby for long periods of time; or you are one of the very few women who do not have enough milk or adequate nipples.

Remember, you can try breast-feeding and change your mind or even shorten the time you planned to breast-feed.

Breast-Feeding Advantages
⇝ *For Baby.* Experts say that mother's milk is the ideal food. It is easily digested and causes no allergies. Antibodies that prevent certain infections and diseases are passed to the baby until his or her immune system is in operation. Mother's milk helps with bowel movements, and the baby cannot overeat since nature sets the limits. If the mother is healthy, there are no disadvantages to a baby in breast-feeding.

⇝ *For Mother.* The method is convenient and economical. It requires only well-fitting nursing bras with washable or disposable pads unless a pump or creams become necessary. The mother needs to continue eating a healthy diet and taking the same vitamins she took while pregnant. Breast-feeding helps in bringing the mother's body back to its pre-pregnancy shape and may even help in weight loss. The mother develops a special intimacy with the new baby that brings both of them much satisfaction.

Breast-Feeding Disadvantages

↪ *For Mother.* Some new mothers do not want to breast-feed because of embarrassment. Other reasons given are: (1) lack of clothes that open for easy feeding; (2) being more tied down to baby; (3) having little or no vaginal fluid while nursing; and (4) discomfort of the actual nursing.

Bottle-Feeding Advantages

↪ *For Baby.* Babies do grow successfully on formula even though it is not a perfect match to their mother's milk and does not contain antibodies.

↪ *For Mother.* A mother who bottle-feeds her baby may be more at ease and less tied down. The father and other family members may share the responsibility and pleasure of feeding the baby. Physically, the mother's menstrual cycle returns to normal sooner.

Bottle-Feeding Disadvantages

↪ *For Baby.* A bottle-fed baby tends to have more gas cramps and spit up more often. Health risks from bacteria in the milk must be guarded against.

⇨ *For Mother.* The use of a bottle does not give the mother and the baby the closeness of breast-feeding. Much of this nurturing can be regained, however, if the mother or caregiver holds the baby at every feeding. The convenience of bottle-feeding depends on whether prepared, powdered, or concentrated formula is used.

How to Breast-Feed

Your baby should be put to your breast as soon after child-birth as possible to stimulate the sucking reflex and encourage your milk supply. Do not be discouraged if the baby only nuzzles or licks the first time; some babies are too tired from childbirth to nurse. Feed the baby every one to three hours, or eight to eighteen times per twenty-four-hour day. This will satisfy baby and increase your milk supply.

Use both breasts and start with a different one each time. Burp baby between breasts and after the last one. Lengthen the sucking time on each breast as baby grows and the number of feeding times decreases.

For a head start on health, breast-feed your baby for a year. Or you can wean him or her to the bottle at four months or to the cup between nine and fifteen months. For practice and in case you must be away from home, introduce your baby to a bottle of warm breast milk once or twice a day.

If you breast-feed, avoid alcohol, any drugs not approved by the baby's doctor, excessive caffeine, and cigarettes.

Collecting and Storing Breast Milk

You can express milk and store it in the refrigerator for twenty-four hours or freeze it for one to two weeks. Freezing may destroy some of its immunities.

Begin with clean hands, equipment, and plastic container. Relax to let your milk down. Use a pump, massage, or warm towels to release the milk. If you freeze the milk, thaw it slowly in cold or warm water for six to eight hours, as heating can destroy additional immunities.

How to Bottle-Feed

Your doctor will probably recommend a commercial formula such as Similac or Enfamil and tell you the proportions to use. The formula is fortified with vitamins and minerals. Ask the doctor if you should give additional vitamins. Never add honey to baby's milk because of the possibility of botulism poisoning. Never add sugar. And under no circumstances should children under age one be given cow's (regular) milk, which contains hard-to-digest proteins, too much sodium, and too little vitamin E and zinc. Breast milk or baby formula must be used. Baby formula is cow's milk that has been specially prepared for your baby.

Transition Stage—Four to Six Months

Adding solid food to a baby's diet is a very important event. The foods you select can in part determine your baby's tastes in food as an adult. Offer a variety of nutritious foods and avoid too much sugar and all junk foods. Even if you do not like some vegetables or fruits, offer them to your little one. Try not to show distaste, which will discourage him or her. Give the baby an opportunity to try and enjoy the new foods.

Add one new food at a time and watch for signs of allergies such as rashes, vomiting or diarrhea, nasal congestion, or even a change in amount of fussiness. If the baby is allergic, do not try the food again until he or she is at least twelve months old.

Start with cereal first. Use the baby's usual milk to prepare it. If necessary, add fruit for taste. Mix only a teaspoon of cereal the first time; you may need even less. Most of it may be returned by the little one's tongue. Remember that eating solid food is a new experience. Let it be a happy, learning one.

Two to four weeks after cereal, start adding stewed fruits at any two feedings during the day. These can be prepared at home or purchased in jars. A variety of fruits are available, including applesauce, peaches, pears, apricots, plums, and prunes. Bananas need not be stewed, just mashed. The baby probably will eat only half a jar at first. Do not feed from the jar, and store the remainder in the refrigerator. Now is a good time to add finger foods such as crackers and toast strips, but watch the baby carefully to prevent choking.

Two to four weeks later, add vegetables. Offer strained string beans, peas, squash, carrots, beets, and sweet potatoes. As meats are added, avoid products like hot dogs and bologna that contain nitrites. By one year the baby's diet will be similar to that of the family, and it is time to begin changing to adult food plus milk in a cup.

Hints for Solid Foods

⮑ Do not expect your baby to like all foods.

⮑ Select a plastic spoon that is small enough for the baby's mouth.

↝ During the first feedings of solid foods, give the milk first. The baby may refuse the solid food because he or she does not yet see it as a way of relieving hunger.

↝ Do not use a feeder or plunger. They do not allow baby to learn the skills of eating.

↝ Adjust the schedule for adding solid foods. Some babies are ready for solid foods as early as two months.

↝ Watch for contamination of baby-food jars. The lid should "pop" when you open it to show freshness.

↝ Always refrigerate jars that have been opened.

↝ Avoid foods that can choke babies such as carrot sticks, nuts, and hard candy.

↝ Use single foods rather than mixtures. Mixtures are less nutritious and cannot be counted as a meat unless labeled "high meat."

↝ Expect a mess. Use a bib for baby and place newspaper under the chair. You may not want to get dressed to go out before feeding baby. Enjoy the new experience with your little one.

Drinking from a Cup

Start your baby practicing with a cup as early as nine months. Give small sips and expect more liquid to be on your baby than in him or her. By fifteen to eighteen months he or she will hold the cup with great skill.

Diet, Disease, and Future Health Problems

The eating habits humans form as infants and children may well increase the chances of health problems in later life.

Obesity

More than one-third of Americans were classified as obese in 1994 by the American Medical Association (AMA), and one-quarter of American children were classified as obese that year as well. The AMA defines adult obesity as having a body weight that is twenty percent greater than the highest healthy weight for your gender and height. For children, the definition and formula are more complex. Ask your doctor about your baby's body mass index, or BMI, a formula that takes into consideration the child's height, weight, age, and gender to determine if the child is seriously overweight. For children, being overweight is usually not a health problem unless the condition is severe or linked to an illness. Overweight children may be more self-conscious about their bodies and should never be told they are "fat" or that they have a "problem."

A body gains weight when it consumes more energy in the form of food and drink than it spends in the form of activity, over time. Determining and controlling the amount of food a person consumes is a problem for many people. Emotions, eating disorders, exercise level and frequency, and the kinds of food eaten greatly impact the quantity that one eats. Controlling the rate at which a person's body burns energy is also a problem for people who are not able to exercise regularly due to physical problems or work schedules. Another factor, even less controllable, is genetics. Research has identified at least two genes linked to obesity. One may prevent the stomach from feeling satisfied or full. The other may slow the rate at which the body uses the food it eats. But it is not certain that any person with these genes must remain overweight no matter what he or she does. Regular exercise may help. No matter what genes a child receives from his mother and father, he or she has a strong chance of inheriting their eating and exercise habits, good and bad.

Dental Problems
The problem of decaying teeth is often food-related. Children and adolescents are most likely to develop cavities. Brushing after each meal is helpful. But most of all, parents must help children develop good snacking habits. Sugary candies are bad for the teeth; however, most of the cavities at this age are caused by soft drinks and starchy foods.

High Blood Pressure, Heart Disease, and Diabetes
Prevention begins in childhood. High blood pressure is one of the most common problems of adults and adolescents. Prevention lies in lower salt intake, weight control, and a low-fat diet. High blood pressure can lead to heart disease, stroke, and kidney failure. Diabetes is increasing with the rise in obesity. It is important to limit the intake of sugar and maintain an average body weight. Babies, children, and adults each have different nutritional requirements. Follow your doctor's guidelines.

The key to good health is staying informed about nutrition. Your understanding of the relationship between diet and disease is important. How do you guide your family's diet? How do you change old eating habits? It is difficult but not impossible. Parents who work are not with their children to guide their snacking. The children eat at the school cafeteria, at relatives' or friends' houses, and at places such as vending machines and fast-food restaurants. When the child eats away from home, the parent is not sure about the total calories consumed and the nutritional value of the food. Your control is at home. You can influence your child's lifelong eating habits in four ways: (1) By the foods you make available at home. Plan, shop, and prepare good snacks. (2) By not having junk food in the house. (3) By educating other family members and baby-sitters on the foods you allow your child to eat. (4) By modeling good eating habits.

Think and Talk About

Jaime's toddler, Suella, wants attention and is crying again. Jaime gives her some sweet fruit juice and cookies in front of the television to calm her down. "Now I can finish my work," Jaime thinks. This pattern becomes typical. After six months, the child has become noticeably overweight. At Suella's three-year checkup, the doctor recommends that Jaime take care not to feed Suella too many sweets and fruit juices. Since Jaime will start a new job in a few weeks, she must find day care for her daughter. When looking for a provider, Jaime is careful to ask what kind of snacks are served and what sweets, if any, come with lunchtime meals. "Are peanut butter and jelly sandwiches ever given for lunch? How often?" she asks.

Finally she finds a center with a good nutrition policy and a lot of indoor and outdoor play space. Jaime also decides to spend at least thirty minutes every other day in a physical activity (even walking to the store will do) with Suella and to serve more fruit instead of cookies and juice.

How did Jaime's attitude toward her crying daughter influence the kind of food she fed to her? If work limits Jaime's time, how could she nevertheless make sure her child eats the right kind of food? How do you think the change in Jaime's and Suella's lifestyle (new job and day care) will affect Suella's weight and nutrition?

Help with Food Costs

If you are not making or receiving enough money to take care of ordinary needs such as providing a home, food, and clothing for your child, there are welfare programs and agencies that can help. If providing an adequate diet for your child is difficult or impossible, check on the following programs:

TANF—Temporary Assistance to Needy Families replaced AFDC (Aid to Families with Dependent Children) as the public program that offers cash and day-care assistance to low-income parents with children. TANF provides financial help while encouraging parents to find work. Most states place a time limit on the duration of cash assistance, and some may require a number of hours of work each week in exchange for cash benefits.

Food Stamps—These are coupons to be spent on groceries. People qualify for this assistance based on income.

WIC—This organization provides cheese, milk, juices, etc. for women, infants, and children who are at risk of nutritional deficiency because of inadequate income.

Head Start—An early education program for minority children with special language needs or children who qualify because of low income. Lunch and snacks are provided.

School Lunches—A program providing free or reduced-price lunch and breakfast at school.

Where do you apply for government help? If family or friends cannot help you find the right agency, consult a minister, social worker, or school counselor. The telephone book is also a good source of information. Look under city, state, and county government. Depending on the kind of help you need, look for titles such as Human Resources, Mental Health, or Family Services. The help is there. Reach out when you need it—and when your child needs it.

Think and Talk About

Special Obstacles for Teen Parents Concerning Health

- ➷ **Teen parents are in the adolescent stage of human development.**

- ➷ **Fertility levels of teen parents are higher than those of other groups.** Without good nutrition, the health of the teen mother and the baby are at

135

stake: Excessive or inadequate weight gain of mothers and low birth weight in babies are the main problems in adolescent pregnancies. Fad dieting, overeating, junk-food diets, and eating disorders also affect teen nutrition.

The Mother: Adolescent girls need good nutrition for their own growth spurt to adult size. The growth spurt combined with pregnancy or one pregnancy followed by another results in additional nutritional needs.

The Baby: Without additional nutrients for the adolescent mother, there is a good chance that the baby will have low birth weight. In the United States in 1996, babies born to mothers age nineteen and under (all teen mothers) were 26 percent more likely to be of low birth weight than babies born to mothers age twenty and older. Babies born to mothers age fourteen and under were 45 percent more likely to be low birth weight. If your child is born at a low birth weight, the doctor will tell you if your baby needs special feedings or nutrients to help him or her catch up.

Note: Low birth weight is defined as fewer than 2,500 grams at birth.

Start today. Follow your doctor's orders on nutrition and additional vitamins and minerals during pregnancy. Monitoring your eating habits is important in pregnancy and to your general good health. It is also important to the kind of model and teacher of nutrition you will be for your child.

Keeping Your Child Safe

Accidents are the leading cause of death and injury among children and young adults. *A childproof household and constant supervision by a careful, watchful parent or caregiver are keys to preventing many accidents.* As your child grows, so does his or her ability to reach out to the world. Keeping the exploring child safe takes planning and action. Decisions about childproofing the home must be made and talked over with the entire family. For a home to be childproof, every person who lives there or takes care of the child must be aware of the potential for accidents. All of the childproofing you do will be useless if someone else is careless. If someone uses a household cleaning material and leaves it in your child's reach, walks away to get a diaper and leaves the baby unattended on the bed or couch, or forgets to close a door or gate, an accident may happen. It takes only one mistake, a few short seconds, and a rolling-over baby or a fast little pair of hands or feet to cause a serious accident.

Think . . . Talk . . . Plan

As you read this chapter, start making the easier changes needed in your house and yard. Make a list of the changes that you will need help completing. Plan your talk with family members and caregivers about your child's safety. Devise ways to keep them thinking about your child's safety. Remind everyone who cares for your child that childproofing the home does not take the place of super-vision. Parents and caregivers must always be on guard and alert.

Safety in the Child's World

Plan Fun and Safe Play Areas. Provide areas inside and outside the house that are totally childproof. Remove any items that are not play-safe for your child and include bar-riers such as fences and gates to prevent the child from leaving the area. A play-safe area allows you to supervise and prevent accidents while doing your household or outdoor work. You may even have time to sit back and enjoy watching your child at play. *The child and parent need time and places where the child can play without being scolded or constantly moved from one spot to another.* The child can play and learn in a play-safe envi-ronment without making a mistake or being disturbed. The parent can join in the play or relax and watch.

Give Your Child Safe Playthings. Toys and ordinary house-hold items are the tools of learning for children. Accidents happen when children are given toys or items that they are not ready for or that were not made to be child-safe. You probably have heard of fathers who purchase a baseball glove or football for a newborn son. Parents, friends, and relatives may give the child toys that are safe but not if given to the child before he or she is ready. Most

138

educational and quality toys provide guidelines based on safety and the age at which a child will be interested in and learn from the toy. As you purchase toys, keep in mind that all children are different. Each one grows and learns in small steps and large spurts. A parent must be the expert and use the guidelines to decide when the child is ready for a toy. Watch for consumer reports to find out if toys are being removed from the market because they are not safe.

Think and Talk About

Read and compare the following experiences of a parent and her child. A toddler learns by exploring and touching new things. But she is not yet able to imagine all of the potential dangers that lurk in her house. How can a tired parent remember to secure every "off-limits" place in her house? How does this parent set rules for her toddler? What does the parent do to make sure that her daughter's desire to learn new things is satisfied? After her child breaks a rule, what does the parent realize about the child's interests?

Sally is a carpenter and often brings her tools home, where she and her three-and-a-half-year-old daughter, Turquoise, live. Turquoise is fascinated with all the colors and shapes in the toolbox. Sometimes her mom opens the box to show Turquoise all of the different tools. But most of the time Sally is tired when she comes home after working hard. Then she places her toolbox on the floor of the closet.

Turquoise likes to explore. She knows where to find the tools. One day she enters the closet before Sally notices. She takes a spray paint can and goes outside to play. Before long Sally hears a cry and runs outside to find her daughter covered in black paint and frightened by a small cut on her finger. Sally realizes that she had forgotten to lock the closet and set it as an off-limits place in the house.

Sally knows that her daughter loves to watch her use her tools. When Sally does chores or fixes something around the house, Turquoise always watches and asks to help. For now, Sally has to say, "No Turquoise, these tools are for adults only." But to encourage Turquoise to develop an interest in tools and building things, Sally has decided to save and buy her daughter a high-quality building block set with a range of sizes and shapes of wooden blocks. As Turquoise gets older, Sally will add new, smaller pieces so that the gift will remain stimulating. Sally and Turquoise will be able to work together on simple projects at first and then Turquoise will learn to build on her own. In a few years, Sally will teach her daughter to use some of her tools. For now, the building block set is a safe alternative. When Sally gives her daughter the gift four months later, Turquoise can't stop playing with it. Sally loves the set as well since she can use the shapes to create models of her real-life construction projects. Now after work, mother and daughter spend time together with the block set.

Now think about a toy you might soon purchase for your child. Ask yourself the same questions. Will your child be interested? Is he or she ready? Will the child be safe?

Does your house have areas that should be off-limits to a child? How can a child's desire to learn and explore new things be balanced with safety? Can you be too strict with dangerous tools? Can you create situations in which your child learns to respect dangerous situations and learns from them? How can these boundaries be moved as your child grows older?

Examine Toys for Small Parts and Sharp Edges. Purchase toys that do not have small parts or sharp edges that can injure your child. Make sure eyes, buttons, wheels, and other items attached to toys are secure. Repair or discard toys that become dangerous.

Plan and Save for Quality Toys. Plan ahead to buy the toys your child needs to grow and learn. Save for the purchase of educational toys. Avoid buying an inexpensive toy each time you have a little money to spare or when grocery shopping. There are three reasons not to start this habit. First, your child begins to expect a toy every time you enter a store. Second, the toys are often unsafe and break easily. Third, the toys are not designed to be learning tools.

Keep a list of needed items with affordable prices for when someone asks, "What does he or she need?" On birthdays and other special occasions, ask friends and family to chip in to buy one needed toy. Help your child understand that everyone contributed to the purchase of the toy or piece of equipment. Help the child save for toys with a piggybank. Family and friends can add coins instead of purchasing inexpensive toys. If some adults continue to purchase toys, talk with them about the importance of safety and educational value. If someone gives your child an unsafe toy, throw it away. If a toy is not appropriate for your child's age, put it away for later. Your child's safety comes first.

Living in an Adult World

Place Poisonous Materials Out of Reach. Dangerous poisons ranging from ordinary aspirin and prescription drugs to bleach and bug sprays must be placed out of a child's reach. Small children open cabinets and climb to get to shelves. Their nosiness never seems to end. Curiosity takes them to things and places that we think are just out of reach. They will eat and drink from anything that they can get open. Little ones have been known to drink the last drops from a bottle that has just been thrown away. They may drink substances with terrible odors such as cleaning materials, kerosene, furniture polish, or insecticide. Parents can never be too careful. To keep your child absolutely safe, you must keep poisonous materials locked up.

Store Yard, Household, and Hobby Tools Properly. Many items used around the house, in the yard, or for your hobbies can be dangerous to children. Maybe you do needlepoint or sew clothing for the family. As you prepare meals, you use a knife or meat fork. You may have a manicure set, screwdrivers for working on household appliances and cars, or pens and pencils for writing or sketching. In the wrong hands—the small hands of children—ordinary items can be dangerous.

Think and Talk About

Sharp Objects. Picture in your mind a baby holding on to a small table for support, a child practicing the new skill of walking, or a child running to meet a friend. Now change those pictures to include an ordinary sharp item left within reach of each one. The picture changes if the child picks up a pencil, knitting needle, dart, screwdriver, or pair of scissors. All sharp objects must be placed out of children's reach when not in use or under the control of an adult.

Small Items. Babies and young children put most things in their mouths. Small items can be swallowed or cause a child to choke. If placed in the nose or ears, these items are hard to remove and may cause discomfort or damage. Many items you use daily are small or have small parts. Start naming them and you will be amazed—coins, small hard candy, buttons, rings, marbles for Chinese Checkers, pegs on a cribbage board, and on and on.

Areas Needing Barriers. If there is a possibility that a child can get into a dangerous area, neither warning him or her nor relying on your supervision will do. What areas in your home need barriers for the protection of your child? Is there danger of falling out of a window or down a flight of stairs? Do you have an open heater or a fireplace? Are electrical outlets and wiring uncovered or within reach of the child?

Do you leave coffeepots or handles of pots and pans within reach? What are the dangers if your child gets outside alone? Traffic? A swimming pool next door? For the safety of your child, use gates, fences, and other barriers.

Vehicle Safety—Seat belts and Car seats! One of your first purchases for baby should be a new or used car seat or carrier. Make sure that it meets safety guidelines and follow the instructions for installing it in your car. Place your child in the car seat to go home from the hospital. Never, never allow your child to ride any other way in any vehicle until he or she becomes "seat-belt size." Demand that your young riders buckle up before the car moves. Do not allow others to take your child in a vehicle without a car seat or seat belt. Model the importance of seat belts by buckling up yourself. The child will be safe in case of an accident and so will you.

Water, Water, Water! Drowning is the second most common cause of preventable, injury-related death among children in the United States, where about 1,000 such fatalities occur each year. In sunny states like California, Florida, and Arizona, it is the leading cause. Private house pools and complex-style pools (in apartment buildings or condominiums, for example) are the sites of most of these drownings. Although public, hotel, health club, and YMCA pools and beaches usually have lifeguards, any body of water, no matter how small or well-supervised, can be deadly. Never leave a young child unattended in a bath, near the toilet, or in a kiddie pool, even for a minute. If you live in a complex with pool, or your neighbor's house has a pool, insist that an isolation fence be installed. This type of fence separates the house or building from the pool, can't be climbed, and features a self-closing latching gate. Above-ground pools should have a locked ladder and steps. All pools should have a five-foot-high fence rather than a chain-link fence. Deck furniture should never be placed next to the fence and gate alarms should be installed. In addition, pool alarms that signal if anything falls into the water prevent many drownings each year. When in the water, you and your child want to play safely. The National Safety Council recommends that you never leave your child unattended near the water. Always use approved personal floatation devices, or lifejackets, rather than inflatable toys.

Emergency Information

Be prepared to make an emergency call. Copy and complete this form now. Post it permanently near your telephone for the use of all family members, guests, and baby-sitters. If you do not have a telephone, place this form where it can easily be seen and removed to take to a telephone in an emergency. Tape coins to the emergency list of telephone numbers if you have to use a pay telephone.

EMS OR AMBULANCE SERVICE _____

FIRE DEPARTMENT _____

POISON CONTROL_____

POLICE DEPARTMENT _____

DOCTOR _____

DENTIST _____

WORK NUMBERS OF ADULTS TO CONTACT:
NAME   PLACE OF BUSINESS   NUMBER

_____   _____   _____

_____   _____   _____

_____   _____   _____

OTHER IMPORTANT CONTACTS AND NUMBERS

_____

_____

Think and Talk About

Special Problems for Teens Concerning Child Safety

> ⇨ *Teen parents are in the adolescent stage of human growth and development.* Adolescence is a time of erratic behavior. The teen may be agreeable today and disagreeable tomorrow, or the teen may take responsibility one day and not the next. When it comes to their child's safety, teen parents have to take a giant step toward adult responsibility. Like all other parents, they must be constantly alert to the dangers that may produce accidents. Care must be taken in childproofing the home. Supervision must be constant. Toys and items for play and learning must be selected carefully. Accidents take seconds; injuries last a lifetime. Death is final.

The Importance of
Child Care

Choosing a caregiver is an extremely important decision that you must make at some point. As an adult you will have other commitments, such as a job, your education, or a career, that you would like to fulfill so that you can keep growing and developing as an individual. While pursuing these interests, you will entrust the care of your child to another adult or to a day care center. Your own self-esteem and self-image will play a big part in who you choose as an appropriate person to watch over your child. Your personal growth and maturity has a direct impact on the way you treat and raise your child. Perhaps you just need time off from being a full-time parent. In fact, occasional relief time spent away from the baby will improve your time spent with the baby.

The caregiver you choose must be somebody you trust completely with your child. This person or center will provide all the care, security, and companionship that you yourself would otherwise provide to the baby. Can this person, for instance, be trusted to feed your child at an unscheduled time if your child feels hungry at an unusual time? Is the person intelligent enough to react quickly during a medical or other emergency? Will the caregiver be allowed to enforce some amount of discipline on the child? Can he or she read to the baby and provide enough mental stimulation while you are away? Is the person capable of distracting the child when he or she is fussy and restless? Rely on your instincts to decide if the person or center suits your and your child's needs.

Kinds of Caregivers

Caregivers can be relatives, sitters, or workers in a family day care center or parent co-op. Some people can afford a housekeeper-caregiver. Most of us have to depend on good friends, parents or relatives, family day care in someone's home, or a day-care center. (Caution: Family day-care centers are not always reported to regulating agencies, nor do all states regulate them adequately. Parents may be the only ones examining them and deciding on the quality of care given.) Some parents have established their own co-op centers where parents either hire a caregiver or take turns sharing the job of watching the children. Sharing the care of the children gives the parents time with their own children. This system can be inexpensive and a learning opportunity for the parents and kids involved.

Steps to Take in Choosing a Person or Center

1. If you have decided to have a baby-sitter or nanny take care of your child, you need to be sure that you have chosen the right person. Don't be hasty in making your choice. Consult the baby's pediatrician for tips on sitters. Your church, synagogue,

or other religious institution also might have suggestions for people and agencies to contact. Other
possible leads in your search for a good sitter
include the local hospital and nursery school
teachers. Since molestation and child abuse are
two increasingly important issues of concern to
parents, you may be considering videotaping the
nanny or sitter alone with the child to see how the
person interacts with the child when no one else
is around. Be sure to hire your nanny on a proba-
tionary basis to see how your child reacts to having a nanny.

After hiring your baby-sitter, you may still wonder about what happens during the day when you
are away. Maybe your child has complained to
you about the sitter. Or maybe you have noticed a
change in your child's personality. For these or
other reasons, you may consider videotaping the
nanny or sitter alone with your child. It is perfectly
legal to operate a hidden camera anywhere,
including your own home, as long as you do not
record any audible conversations. But there are
issues of trust involved. How would a professional
and quality nanny feel if she knew that you were
secretly watching her as she worked? You should
ask yourself if you have real reasons to believe
that there is a problem.

"Nannycams," as they are known in the video
industry, are expensive to rent or buy. If you install
a hidden surveillance camera in your home, do
not position it in the bathroom or bedroom.
Parents who want advice about the most current

rules and laws concerning hidden cameras should contact their local chapter of the American Civil Liberties Union (ACLU), the National Association of Nannies, or a nannycam seller such as Baby Watch.

2. ***Carefully consider the caregiver's personality.*** You need to spend as much time as possible with your potential caregiver to be absolutely certain that you are happy with your choice. Ask the person about his or her views on child care and discipline. What kind of stimulation would he or she provide for the child? What does the person think a child of your child's age needs most? Was he or she punctual or late for the interview? Will the caregiver be able to work during bad weather conditions? Does he or she have children of his or her own? Why did the person leave his or her last job? How healthy is the person? Has he or she had a TB test recently? Is he or she physically capable of handling the job? Does he or she seem intelligent? And do you think you will be compatible together in raising your child?

3. ***Interview more than one person.*** As you interview the caregiver, consider the following questions: Does the person like and enjoy children? Can he or she show love? Can he or she make quick, good decisions? Does this person seem to have too many of his or her own problems? Can this person care for children in a controlling, guiding way without being too severe?

150

4. *Visit more than one day care center.* The first thing you want to be sure of when looking for a day care center is whether it is a legitimate, licensed operation. Does the center have a trained and experienced staff, or is it a makeshift operation posing as a professional center? Does the center enforce strict health and safety regulations regarding sanitation? Does it have strict safety rules for ensuring full protection for the child? Do the caregivers encourage the children to care about and respect one another?

5. *Take your child with you to see how responsive the caregiver is to the child.* If the child is "in the caregiver's way" during the interview, think what it will be like when you leave your child alone with the person. Check your child's reactions to the person and the environment.

6. *Look at the surroundings.* Are they clean? Do they have some kind of order? Are there opportunities for children to play, explore, and learn? Is there room to eat, sleep, and play comfortably?

7. *Ask about the caregiver's policy on sharing of information.* Does the caregiver want to know about your child's special needs? Will you be kept informed of your child's progress or needs?

8. *Compare costs of services provided.* Costs include fees for late pick-up, times available for care, type of food served, learning opportunities, and willingness and space to take ill children.

151

After You Have Selected a Caregiver

1. *Help your child adjust gradually to the new schedule and surroundings.* Take your child for short periods at first. Return for pick-up at the time promised. Your child will soon learn that you will return each time. He or she will feel safe.

2. *Understand that there may be some fussiness.* You can help with this. Often the parent is the one having trouble saying goodbye. Give your child a positive message by limiting your goodbyes and leaving quickly and cheerfully.

3. *Communicate with the caregiver.* Share events that happen at home that may affect your child's day. Check on your child's progress once a week.

4. *Try not to be jealous if your child wants to stay with the person or at the center.* Realize that this is a good sign. Your child likes the new caregiver and feels comfortable in the environment.

5. *Continue to monitor the care your child receives.* Feel free to ask questions until you feel sufficiently informed.

6. *Do not hesitate to remove your child if your first choice of a caregiver is not the right one.* You have made a mistake only if you continue to take your child to an unsatisfactory caregiver or center.

152

7. ***Keep an updated list of numbers for all caregivers in case of emergency.*** Leave instructions in writing for baby-sitters in your home. Use the following example to set up your own message to the sitter.

Information for the Sitter
(Give full name of each child and his or her nickname.)

CHILD   Medications   Allergies   Other concerns

_____

_____

_____

_____

BABY'S SCHEDULE—BATHING, NAPS, FEEDING
INFORMATION/BOTTLES AND SOLID FOODS

_____

_____

_____

_____

EMERGENCY NUMBERS:
PARENT _____
Location _____ Number _____
PARENT _____
Location _____ Number _____
DOCTOR'S NAME _____
Office _____ Home _____
Emergency Number _____
DENTIST'S NAME _____
Office _____ Emergency Number _____

POISON CONTROL _____
EMERGENCY CLINIC/HOSPITAL _____
IN CASE OF FIRE _____
PERSON(S) to call in case of emergency if parents cannot be reached:
(1) Name _____ Address _____
Home Number _____ Work Number _____
Relationship _____
(2) Name _____ Address _____
Home Number _____ Work Number _____
Relationship _____

OTHER: (Include information about safety concerns, food for the sitter, special arrangements about television watching, etc.)

Think and Talk About

Part of learning and growing is knowing when a mistake has been made and correcting it. We all make mistakes. The following report of one beginner's successes and mistakes may help you. As you read about her experiences with caregivers, review the information in this chapter. Decide what you would or would not have done in the same situation.

In the first example that follows, the parent's choice of day care center was suited more to her own needs than those of her child. The center that the mother's friends recommended was out of the way and would prevent her from working overtime. The extra overtime salary was definitely needed in their household, so she chose a day care center that was close to where she worked. Unfortunately, at this center, the child was hit quite often by other children. Apparently some of the children in the school behaved very poorly and the day care staff did not adequately curb their bad behavior. In addition, the day care workers themselves would hit the children as a means of "disciplining" them. Respect for other children was not taught. As a result, the center was frequently chaotic, and a poor place for learning how to get along with others. One day the child came home with a large bruise on his arm. One of the other children, who was a year older, had taken a toy from him and knocked him down. When he pushed back and tried to reclaim the toy, one of the caregivers saw him and roughly pinched his arm. The caregiver had not seen how the fight had started and had not taken the time to learn the truth. Why was her behavior inappropriate? First, because an adult should not physically hurt a child. Second, the caregiver had wrongly jumped to a conclusion; of course, even if her conclusion had been right, she should not have punished the child the way she did. Needless to say, the mother was forced to find a safer and better day care center for her child.

In the second example to follow, a teen parent had to continue her part-time job to make ends meet, so her sister graciously agreed to babysit the child on the days that she didn't have classes at school. However, this schedule soon began to affect the sister's performance in school, and so the parent was forced to enroll her child into day care. The parent took all the possible leads she could get when looking around for a good day care center. She found a center that was not too far away and had a good reputation. The *parent went there with her sister and the baby to have a look at it. The facility was warm and inviting as soon as she entered it. It was clean and well maintained and had various kinds of educational toys and other learning materials. The director, a kind and gentle woman, lifted the child in her arms as she showed them around. There were enough helpers on hand to give the child a good deal of personal attention. Some of the other children came forward to befriend the child as soon as they saw him. The attitude of the center was to make the newcomer feel as welcome as possible. Some of the workers were well-versed in basic medical care like CPR for children in case of emergencies. The baby seemed to accept the place instantly, so much so that he didn't want to leave in the evenings.*

In the third example here, the day care center was chosen on the basis of a healthy atmosphere and the possibility for learning. Parents and children were required to interview with the director and at least one of the caregivers. Children were allowed to try out the learning materials after class hours. Everyone involved—the parent, the child, and the director—had to agree that this was a good place for the child. The child continued at the preschool until he began kindergarten.

Think and Talk About

Special Obstacles for Teen Parents Regarding Caregivers

> ➭ *A limited number of people are available to share the responsibility of parenting with the*

teen parent. Teen parents continue their education, have a job, or just need time out. The teen parent may have to look outside his or her family circle for caregivers for the child. The information in this chapter should help in making a decision.

⮑ ***Teen parents are in the adolescent stage of human growth and development.*** Teen parents must be careful that the insecurity that comes with being an adolescent does not get in the way of their child's adjustment to caregivers. The child's attachment to the caregiver can cause any parent to be jealous. The teen parent's feelings of insecurity can make it worse. It is important to help the child develop a trusting relationship with the person who shares his or her care.

Teen parents often find themselves interviewing caregivers who are older and more experienced than they are. These parents must keep in mind that as the employer, they have a choice.

⮑ ***Fertility levels of teen parents are higher than those of other groups.*** Additional children increase the cost of care by sitters or at centers. Friends or relatives who are willing to care for one child might not want to care for two. Teen parents may have to drop out or postpone their education or career plans when the second or third child arrives. Family planning help in choosing to postpone or have a second or third child is available and may be important to your future. The resource section of this book will guide you to agencies that provide planned parenthood services.

> *Life plans change.* You may have to move else-where because of a new job opportunity, to go to college, etc. Even though such a step forward is an exciting one, it may mean that you will have to arrange for childcare in a new community. The thought of moving your child from a childcare sit-uation in which he or she is happy may make you both unhappy.

> *Family structure and lifestyles change.* Becoming a parent changed your life. The adolescent need to be free and independent became more difficult to achieve. Dependent on your family or welfare agencies for support, you realized that you are not really free and self-supporting. You are not the only provider for your child; to become indepen-dent, you will have to settle for temporary support. You will have to complete your education or train-ing and enter the job market. But the independent and good feelings gained are worth the wait and hard work. Becoming a self-reliant adult and provider for your child is a major success. Without putting in effort and time, you might be dependent forever on your parents or welfare.

Child Abuse: Hurt That Lasts a Lifetime

Child abuse is a growing problem in the United States, and the sooner that parents are aware of how it begins, the better prepared they are to prevent the problem from getting out of hand. About one million children were the victims of substantiated or indicated child abuse and neglect in 1996, an approximate 18 percent increase since 1990. An estimated 1,077 child abuse and neglect fatalities occurred in the United States in 1996.

REACH, a Texas PTA Children's Program, defines child abuse as "the nonaccidental physical or emotional injury or damage to a child by a person responsible for the child's health or welfare. Child abuse includes physical abuse, sexual abuse, neglect, exploitation, and emotional abuse." Child abuse happens in families of all races, ethnic groups, backgrounds, creeds, socio-economic groups, and marital statuses. Child abuse happens in single and married families, in rich and poor homes, and in black, Hispanic, and Anglo homes. Adults lose control of a situation for one or more of the following reasons: they were abused in childhood, or they are struggling with alcohol or drug abuse, stress due to economic or marital problems, or mental illness.

There are several reasons why children are abused. The most common reason is that the parents of abused

159

children have been abused themselves. Marital, financial, drug, and alcohol problems also increase the risk of some forms of child abuse.

The prevention of child abuse has become a major campaign in the United States over the last few years. Psychologists have found that an abused child is affected for life, and often very seriously. Abused children tend to be insecure, lack confidence, and have a stunted emotional growth. They have problems developing a healthy self-esteem, which in turn affects their relationships with people. However, child abuse certainly can be stopped or rectified as soon as parents recognize the signs of it.

The first sign of potential child abuse is when someone—including a parent—wants to hit the child out of anger and impatience. The child, defenseless and vulnerable, sometimes becomes the punching bag for an adult's frustration. Children, unlike adults, need to be instructed, explained to, and corrected several times before they learn a certain pattern of behavior. Occasionally a parent might choose to spank the child if he or she misbehaves when the child is old enough to understand a rational explanation. Yet a forceful slap or a violent shaking of the child in a moment of impatience that afterward is rationalized as "discipline" can slip into a habit of abuse. This is the telltale sign of the kind of abuse that can get out of hand if it is not noticed and immediately corrected. If you find that you are losing control with your child in this way, do not be afraid to seek help from a counselor or to call Parents Anonymous or Childhelp USA. Contact information for these and other resources is listed in the next section as well as in chapter eighteen.

Child abuse is not necessarily restricted to an adult

beating or punching a child on a regular basis. There are various kinds of abuse.

Types of Abuse

Neglect. Infants are completely dependent upon their parents for survival. Food, clothing, and emotional and physical nourishment are required for infants to be healthy. Children who are left unattended in a home or car or who are given little or no attention are neglected. Colicky babies are neglected if their parents run out of patience and endurance to deal with the problem and leave them at home alone. Neglect is detrimental to the child's health and is potentially fatal. More than 150,000 children in the United States suffered neglect in 1996.

Physical abuse. Physical abuse, as discussed earlier, is the use of unwarranted force on a child. According to a study conducted in 1996, more than 60,000 children in the United States were victims of physical abuse that year. Physical abuse doesn't necessarily mean that the child is badly bruised or cut each time he or she is abused. The indiscriminate use of moderate force on a child is still abuse. In addition, a child is physically abused if he or she is left unprotected from physical harm. Pinching, biting, and hair pulling by an adult is physical abuse. Babies and children pinch, bite, and pull hair, but they are just little children who don't know better.

Sexual abuse. According to a study by the U.S. Department of Health and Human Services, more than

28,000 children in the United States were victims of sexual abuse in 1996. Sexual abuse is any touching of a child's genitals other than for diapering, cleaning, or bathing. Making a child perform sexual acts on him- or herself, other children, or adults is sexual abuse. Molestation is also sexual abuse.

Exploitation. Taking a picture of a naked baby for any reason other than placement in a baby book is not to be done. Some people have exploited children by photographing them in the nude or while involved in sexual acts. These adults pose as friends, friendly neighbors, or club leaders. Protect your child. Know and check on adults with whom you leave your child.

Emotional Abuse. Children deserve a supportive, peaceful environment. Their parents should be their number one supporters. Emotional abuse of a child arises when parents yell, scream, or use put-downs and profane language in front of their child. More than 10,000 children in the United States suffered emotional maltreatment in 1996.

If you find yourself or someone in your household losing control with your child, call a child-abuse hotline immediately:
Parents Anonymous   (909) 621-6184
Provides referrals to local self-help groups for parents and children.
Childhelp USA   (800) 4-A-CHILD / (800) 422-4453
Gives referrals twenty-four hours a day, seven days a week.

If your child is abused, call for help and get counseling for all involved! Help your child to understand that he or she is not at fault. Children who are abused must understand that it is the adult's problem and that they do not deserve such treatment. Remember, child abuse hurts forever. The damage done to a child does not go away when the abuse stops. Without counseling and sometimes even with counseling, the child will carry the scar of child abuse into adulthood. The abused child may become an abusing adult or may have a problem accepting him- or herself as a worthwhile, deserving person.

If you were abused as a child, seek counseling to help with the hurt and to feel better about yourself. Keep in mind that abused children often become abusive adults. You and your child deserve better.

Think and Talk About

Special Obstacles for Teen Parents and Child Abuse

➥ *A limited number of people are available to share the responsibility of parenting with the teen parent.* The need for everyone to have their own time and space is important. Often teen parents are left with the total responsibility of a baby or child without relief time.

➥ *Teen parents are in the adolescent stage of human growth and development.* Teens are still growing and developing. They need to find themselves and feel independent, and these feelings may cause them to be jealous of their own child or feel that their child is in the way.

↪ *Family structure and lifestyles change.* The changes in how and where you live after your baby is born can be stressful. Money for food, clothing, and shelter is in short supply. Extras and entertainment may be out of the question. At a time when you normally would be seeking independence in life, you may have become totally dependent on your parents. The stresses of the family may be taken out on the baby. Teens living at home may also continue to be subjected to abuse by their parents. *Tell someone. Ask for help. Call a hotline. Stop the hurt.*

If you are allowing your frustrations to affect how your child is treated or cared for, ask for relief time; share the care. *Ask for help. Call a hotline. Seek counseling. Stop the hurt.*

Mother Care:
The First Six Weeks

The period that begins with the baby's delivery and lasts for about six to eight weeks is called the postpartum period. For the mother and baby this period has far-reaching importance, since their future health depends on proper rest and care. During this time, the mother's reproductive organs return to normal, the baby becomes a part of the family, and all members of the household must change their roles in the family to cope with the demands of the new baby.

When a woman becomes pregnant, she prepares for and focuses on the changes that pregnancy brings and the delivery of the new baby. Often preparation for the period right after the birth is ignored or focused only on the baby. Not learning about and preparing for her own physical and emotional needs after delivery will limit a new mother's ability to recover physically and cope emotionally with her new responsibilities. The dream of being a good parent can be fulfilled only if she takes care of her own needs. To ignore the bodily and mood changes of the postpartum period may make her new role as mother overwhelming if not impossible.

If you are a new mother, read this chapter for background information. Make a list of any questions you have and ask your doctor or clinician. If you realize that you have a problem that needs medical care, call immediately.

Postpartum Physical Changes

The Uterus

During the beginning of the postpartum period, two physical changes take place in your body. The uterus returns to its former size and milk develops in the breasts. The uterus shrinks from an organ of two to three pounds that held a baby to one of less than two ounces. This process is called *involution*. As the uterus and the pelvic structures return to their former condition, the majority of women feel quite comfortable. After childbirth, massaging the uterus through the abdomen as well as the baby's nursing help stimulate the contractions needed to maintain firmness, help shrinkage, and prevent heavy blood loss. In the hospital, the caregivers should massage the uterus. At home, you continue the massaging. The uterus can be felt between the navel and the pubic bone like a tight muscle the size of a grapefruit that gives a distinct bulge to the lower abdomen. Within a week its weight will diminish by one half; within ten days it is usually so small that it lies entirely in the pelvic cavity and can no longer be felt through the abdominal wall.

The most noticeable phase of involution is the breaking down and casting off of the thickened lining of the uterus. This gives rise to a profuse vaginal discharge called *lochia*. There are variations from person to person, but you can expect a heavy red flow containing substantial amounts of blood mixed with cellular debris for the first four to five days. Three-fourths of the total discharge of about one pint is passed in the first four days. The amount of flow increases on standing or sitting up from a position of lying down.

Breast-feeding also increases the flow. Near the end of the first week the color fades to brown, and becomes light yellow or whitish by about the tenth day. At the end of two to three weeks the discharge disappears almost entirely.

CAUTION: Watch for signs of infection or excessive bleeding. Call your doctor or clinician if the discharge (1) turns red again after it has paled; (2) is as profuse as on the first day of a menstrual period; (3) contains large bloody clots; or (4) has a foul odor.

Lactation

During pregnancy your breasts underwent changes to prepare for providing food for a baby. They secreted *colostrum,* a protein-rich watery liquid that nourishes the baby until milk arrives. The colostrum contains antibodies that protect the baby from certain infections. The milk arrives about three days after delivery, when the baby has had time to recover and is ready for food. You know when the milk comes because the breasts become tighter and the veins stand out. When the baby is put to the nipple, a white, opaque, and sugar-rich liquid known as milk runs out. The fullness of the breasts on the day the milk comes causes some discomfort, especially with first babies. The breasts are tense, hard to the touch, and painful. The coming of the milk is not the problem. Rather, it is the congestion that forms in the surrounding blood vessels when the milk glands begin to function. The discomfort rarely lasts more than forty-eight hours. From that point on the baby's demands control milk production.

Frequent nursing for at least ten minutes on each breast helps. For more relief, apply ice packs and support the breasts with a nursing bra, even in bed. Sagging breasts, which some women experience later in life, can be prevented with support unless they are a family trait. Sagging does not come from nursing a baby but rather from lack of support of the breasts during pregnancy and nursing.

Care of the Nipples and Breasts

Daily care of the nipples is important to breast-feeding. Wash them at least once a day with a clean cloth, soap, and water at the beginning of your bath or shower. If there is a problem with irritation, stop using soap. If your breasts leak, use small sterile pads in your bra. Change them at least twice daily or when they become soaked.

Sore nipples are not unusual during the early days of nursing. Small cracks in the nipples or raw areas cause the soreness. Various healing ointments are available. Early treatment prevents having to interrupt breast-feeding or becoming discouraged and deciding to quit. If an infection is not treated, nursing may have to be suspended for twenty-four to forty-eight hours.

If nursing becomes painful, you must see the doctor and get treatment right away. The minor breast irritations and infection have become *mastitis.* Bacteria from the baby's mouth or your skin have entered the bloodstream. The breasts become painful, extra firm, red in color, and hot to the touch. Fever and chills may develop. The doctor or clinician will prescribe antibiotics.

You should maintain a regular nursing schedule and vary the baby's position while nursing. The nursing will keep the milk ducts from clogging, promote healing, and provide comfort. If the baby does not empty the breasts, use a breast pump to express the milk. If nursing is too painful, the breast pump can be used to express milk for the baby to drink from a bottle.

Non-Breast-Feeding Mothers

If you cannot or choose not to breast-feed, the doctor will give you medication immediately after delivery or within the next few days to stop lactation. The milk may temporarily continue to flow. To help diminish the supply and relieve the discomfort, apply the pressure of a tight-fitting bra or ice packs or take an analgesic.

Afterpains

Occasionally menstrual-like cramps are experienced during the first three days by mothers who have had a previous baby. For first-time mothers, they are not so common. As the uterus contracts to expel small clots, the mother experiences discomfort or pain. This often happens while the baby is nursing. Relaxing and breathing slowly will help. The afterpains mean that your figure is returning to normal, and should stop in a few days.

Perineal Care and Episiotomies

Cleanliness of the perineal area is necessary to prevent infection and promote healing. If a tear occurred during delivery or the doctor performed the surgical procedure called an *episiotomy*, stitches must heal. A doctor performs an episiotomy because it is easier to repair than a tear, it allows the baby's head to pass through, and it speeds the delivery. The incision is made in a straight line from the vagina toward the rectum. Healing takes about four weeks.

For comfort and healing of the incision or tear:

- ↝ Take a sitz bath for twenty minutes three times a day (sit in a shallow tray of warm water placed over the toilet).

- ↝ Stand under a warm shower.

- ↝ Use a heating pad.

- ↝ Use analgesics and creams recommended by your doctor.

- ↝ After you are allowed to take baths, sit in a warm tub of water for twenty minutes.

- ↝ Lie on your side with your knees up to relieve pressure.

- ↝ After healing takes place, try applying hot or cold packs for fifteen to twenty minutes to relieve discomfort.

- ↝ Always wipe from front to back to avoid infection.

- ↝ Do not douche or use tampons.

Share with Your Partner

Discomfort from the incision or tear may be experienced for several months and during intercourse for as long as four months. How will you and your partner help each other with the problem?

Think and Talk About

Remember that a tear might be deeper than the incision of an episiotomy. Realize that some doctors perform an episiotomy routinely even when not necessary. Should you discuss this topic with your doctor or clinician before delivery? The time required to repair the incision may delay mother-infant interaction. How can you avoid or make up for this delay?

Cesarean Birth

The period after Cesarean birth is similar to that after vaginal birth except for the incision and the hospital stay of three to six days. In most cases the involution and lochia are similar.

The surgery lengthens the time it takes to regain strength and resume normal activities. However, you will be asked to get out of bed within twenty-four hours. A little dizzy or lightheaded, you may need some help. Standing upright and moving around will relieve gas pains and speed recovery. Within a week or two, a decision will made about beginning postpartum exercises.

Because of the anesthetic given for surgery, you must work to clear your lungs. Deep breathing and coughing will clear the accumulated mucus and increase lung capacity. This must be repeated every fifteen minutes for the first twenty-four hours; the doctor may then advise you to continue the clearing every thirty minutes for a while.

The need for rest, a nutritious diet, plenty of fluids, and help around the house is even more important after a Cesarean birth. Overexertion must be avoided to prevent excessive bleeding.

Disadvantages expressed by some about Cesarean birth are that the need for sterile surgery prevents immediate viewing and holding of the baby, gives the mother a feeling of inadequacy or disappointment at missing the birth, and often excludes the partner or other family member from what goes on in the operating room.

For women who experience certain health problems before or during labor, however, such as serious diabetes or open herpes sores, Cesarean births can be lifesaving. In other cases—such as when the baby is too large or is in an unusual position, or when the woman's pelvis is too small or her labor is too slow—Cesarean births can prevent serious damage to both the mother and the baby.

Constipation

The doctor does not usually release a new mother from the hospital until she has had a bowel movement. Constipation may be a problem for the first two or three weeks. Lax abdominal muscles, soreness of the perineum, or hemorrhoids can cause the problem. No laxative should be taken without the doctor's approval. Some kinds of laxatives can cause cramps or can be passed to the baby during breast-feeding.

Constipation can be relieved naturally by returning to normal activity, eating fresh fruits and fiber-rich foods, drinking plenty of water, walking, exercising the abdominal muscles, and taking plenty of time when moving the bowels. If pain in the perineal area is a problem, gently pressing toilet tissue at the site of the episiotomy will relieve soreness and decrease fear of pain. If hemorrhoids are the problem, it may help to avoid constipation and to exercise the pelvic floor area with contractions, specifically of the muscles around the anus.

Urination

Most women have no problem with urination after delivery. A new mother should try to urinate every six hours. A full bladder pushes the uterus high in the abdomen and interferes with its contracting. Within twenty-four hours of delivery, a woman is able to use the toilet for urination. Before that time a catheter may have to be used, and then possibly a bedpan. Difficulty in urinating usually is solved by drinking plenty of water, relaxing, or running water in the sink or over the perineum. If simple procedures do not work, catheterization becomes necessary: A small rubber tube is inserted in the bladder to drain the urine.

Personal hygiene is important for preventing vaginal infection. Wash your hands before and after urinating. Pat yourself clean from front to back. Use no wiping motions.

Rest and Relaxation

Childbirth causes fatigue. At no time are rest and quiet needed more than in the early days after delivery. Rest will help you get up sooner. The amount of rest needed depends on how you feel. You should plan on half-an-hour to an hour twice a day. This can be taken when the baby is asleep during the day and by going to bed early to be prepared for night feedings. Take every opportunity to rest, including while feeding the baby. Sit in a comfortable armchair with your feet up or lie down if you are sure you won't fall asleep and drop the baby.

Exercise

Resuming normal activity may be discouraging at first. Your energy level may not return as soon as you expect, but it will come back eventually. Exercising should begin as soon as possible. Some doctors recommend starting very simple muscular movements a day or two after delivery. Others prefer patients to wait up to ten days. If pain is experienced, exercise should be discontinued for a while.

Diet

You may begin eating as soon as you like. Mothers who breast-feed have additional dietary needs. The diet should be nutritious and generous and should include milk between meals and at bedtime. Fluid intake should be increased to three to four quarts daily, with one quart being milk. An additional serving of oranges, grapefruit, or tomatoes is recommended. Include fiber and roughage as well as extra protein in the form of lean meat, eggs, beans, or peas. Continue taking prenatal vitamins and iron.

From Shower to Bath

Focusing so much attention on the baby may cause you to forget yourself. You will feel better if you look well. Your hair, teeth, and skin need the same attention as before you became pregnant. Daily showers generally begin in the hospital as soon you can stand. Sponge baths of the breasts and perineal area are recommended if you are not ready for a shower. Three weeks after delivery or as soon as the doctor permits, you may take tub baths.

Final Examination

Almost all doctors recommend a final visit six weeks to two months after delivery. At this time a complete pelvic examination is given and you are advised about resuming normal activities. This is the time to ask questions: What kind of contraception should be used to space future pregnancies? How soon can tampons be used? When can intercourse be resumed?

Return to Menstruation

There is no set time that menstruation resumes. In women who do not nurse, the time ranges from four to eight weeks to three or four months. Breast-feeding tends to inhibit menstruation; most women who nurse their babies do not menstruate for five or six months and often not until breast-feeding is stopped. Occasionally, however, a mother who is breast-feeding does menstruate.

The first menstrual period after delivery is often profuse, contains clots, and may stop and start again. The second period should be normal.

Personal hygiene during menstruation is important at all times but especially during the postpartum period. You will be wearing sanitary napkins for two to three weeks, and vaginal infection is a possibility. Napkins must be changed often and hands washed before and after. Both the removal of a used napkin and placement of a fresh one should be from front to back.

Some breast-feeding mothers assume that they cannot become pregnant while nursing. They are wrong. The ovaries begin to function again soon after delivery, making pregnancy possible before menstruation resumes.

Intercourse

During the time that intercourse is not safe, partners must remember other ways to show love. Physically affectionate contact such as a back rub can express feelings of love, understanding, and belonging.

Doctors advise new mothers on when to resume intercourse. Six weeks after delivery is average. Most doctors give their approval during the final examination if stitches are healed and the vaginal discharge has stopped. Not all couples wait for the doctor's advice. Before making this decision, the mother should be ready both physically and emotionally. She may take a while to return to her prior level of sexual activity. Her female instincts have become temporarily focused on the baby. She also may have a sore perineum, a lack of help, fatigue, the "baby blues," or a decrease in vaginal lubrication due to hormonal changes.

Contraception

You can conceive again very soon after childbirth. Eighty-five percent of women who are sexually active and do not use birth control become pregnant within one year.

Although no method of birth control except abstinence is effective 100 percent of the time, there are methods that greatly reduce the chances of pregnancy. Use the following information and the advice of your doctor or clinician to make a decision with your partner.

Methods Requiring a Prescription

The Pill includes many brands now widely used. On the whole, the side effects are far reduced from those caused by the Pill of a generation ago. It is a reversible prescription method that requires you to take one pill per day throughout each month. The two main types are the Combined Pill and the Mini-Pill.

↪ **Effectiveness:** If the Pill is taken as prescribed, only three in 100 women will become pregnant during the first year of use. Women who take the Pill correctly every day have less than a 1 percent chance of getting pregnant. The user must adhere strictly to the one-pill-per-day regimen. Missing even one day can disrupt the entire month of protection. The Pill offers no protection against sexually transmitted diseases (STDs).

↪ **Method:** Both types of the Pill work by preventing your ovaries from releasing eggs. More importantly, they increase the amount of mucus that layers the cervix, the place where sperm can fertilize the eggs. They may also prevent unfertilized eggs from attaching to the uterine walls.

↪ **Cost:** Monthly packages of pills cost between $15 and $25, less at a clinic. Medicaid covers the cost, and some types of health insurance may offer partial reimbursement. Also possibly covered is a doctor's examination, which costs at least $35.

↪ *Recommendations:* Most women can take the Pill with few or no problems. Side effects that may stop in a few months include breast tenderness, nausea, spotting between periods, vomiting, or weight gain or loss. Some women who are not sexually active use the Pill to make their menstrual cycle more regular and to reduce severe cramps. Women who smoke or who have diabetes, high levels of blood fats, or high blood pressure should inform their doctors of these situations before starting their prescriptions.

Norplant is a reversible prescription method that requires a large up-front investment but no planning, maintenance or cost for up to five years thereafter. Six small soft capsules are placed under the skin of the upper arm, where they release hormones into the bloodstream of the user.

↪ **Effectiveness:** Fewer than one woman in 1,000 will become pregnant during the first year of use. Left in place, Norplant can prevent pregnancy for up to five years. Norplant offers no protection against sexually transmitted diseases.

↪ **Method:** Receiving Norplant requires a minor surgical procedure performed in the doctor's office or clinic. The doctor inserts six small capsules into a small incision under the skin of your arm. Like the Pill, Norplant delivers a small amount of the hormone progestin into your bloodstream. The hormone helps to control the timing of your ovulation and thickens the layer of mucus covering your cervix.

↪ **Cost:** Norplant costs between $500 and $700 for the exam, implants, and procedure. The insertion will last for up to five years, so the cost per year is about $150. Removal of the capsules before they are used up will add another $100 to $200 to your total cost. Medicaid and many types of health insurance may reimburse all or part of your costs.

↪ **Recommendations:** The side effects of Norplant are minimal. They include irregular intervals between periods, longer menstrual flow, irregular bleeding between periods, or no bleeding for months at a time. Changes in bleeding usually normalize after nine to twelve months. Some other effects to watch for may include headache, dizziness, sore breasts, acne, and weight gain or loss. Norplant is a good choice for women who do not want to have children for a few years.

The Intrauterine Device (IUD) is a small device containing copper or a natural hormone that is inserted into the uterus by a doctor or clinician. Some kinds can be left in place for many years. When her IUD is removed, a woman can become pregnant again immediately.

↪ **Effectiveness:** Fewer than three in 100 women will become pregnant during the first year of use. With continued use the chances decrease even more. Many women use the IUD in conjunction with condoms or spermicidal foam during intercourse. Users must check for the placement of the IUD "string" on a regular basis. IUDs offer no protection against sexually transmitted diseases.

↪ **Method:** IUDs work by preventing fertilization of an egg. They also prevent unfertilized eggs from implanting in the lining of the uterus. When the IUD is in the correct position, a string will be visible to you on examination.

You must regularly check to make sure that the string is in place and visible.

➦ **Cost:** The cost of the initial doctor's exam, insertion, follow-up office visits, and the IUD itself can range from $175 to $450. Prices at clinics are lower, and Medicaid may cover some or all.

➦ **Recommendation**: The IUD may be right for you if you have had a baby, and you have only one sex partner who has sex only with you. It is the most popular method of birth control in the world. But you should definitely not use the IUD if you have a history of pelvic infection or have any disease, such as HIV, that decreases your ability to fight infections.

➦ **Caution:** Some women have reported increased and severe menstrual cramping after having an IUD inserted. There is also concern that the IUD can fall out of position. Pregnancy could then occur. If this happens, a doctor must remove the IUD as soon as possible. In addition, though this is very rare, the IUD can puncture the wall of the uterus, especially during insertion.

Depo-Provera is a synthetic hormone that is injected into the woman's buttocks or arm every twelve weeks. It regulates the menstrual cycle and keeps the ovaries from releasing eggs. It also thickens cervical mucus that keeps sperm from fertilizing the egg.

➦ **Effectiveness:** Only three out of every 1,000 women will become pregnant during the first year of use. Like other non-barrier methods, Depo-Provera provides no protection against sexually transmitted diseases.

➥ *Method:* Every twelve weeks the user must visit a health care facility to receive an injection into her arm or buttock. Protection comes within five hours if the appointment is timed around her period. Hormones regulate her cycle for twelve weeks and keep the ovaries from releasing eggs. They also thicken cervical mucus that keeps sperm from fertilizing any eggs.

➥ *Cost:* The initial exam costs at least $35 (less at a clinic). The first hormone injection costs about $50, but subsequent shots cost less. Medicaid and some HMOs may partially cover the cost of Depo-Provera.

➥ *Recommendations:* A woman who cannot take estrogen can still use this method. The most common side effect is irregular bleeding, but this may last only for the first six to twelve months. After one year the menstrual period may stop. Sore breasts, headache, dizziness, and depression can also occur.

Emergency Hormonal Contraception, also known as the "Morning-After Pill," is a prescription method of birth control for women who believe that their regular method of birth control failed during intercourse. Victims of rape also use this method to ensure that they do not become pregnant. The pills must be taken within seventy-two hours of having unprotected sex.

➥ *Method:* Emergency hormonal contraception is similar to other types of hormone-based birth control. It is used to regulate the menstrual cycle so that any current ovulation will not result in a pregnancy. The user obtains six pills and takes two as soon as possible within seventy-two hours of the risky intercourse. Two more pills are to be taken twelve hours after that. The last two pills are taken only if the user vomits within two hours of taking either the first or the second group of two pills. This "last resort" birth control works because fertilization of the egg does not happen instantaneously after intercourse. The use of this method insures that eggs break down before fertilization can occur.

➭ **Cost:** A clinic exam, prescription, and pills will cost about $50. Coverage by Medicaid and HMOs is unlikely.

➭ **Recommendations:** A woman who believes that her preferred method of birth control has failed should contact a clinic or a Planned Parenthood office if she does not want to get pregnant. It is likely that she will experience side effects such as vomiting, sore breasts, and headache, but no lasting symptoms.

Barrier Methods: The Cervical Cap and the Diaphragm

The **cervical cap** and **diaphragm** are reversible barrier methods of birth control that require a prescription and doctor's office or clinic visit. The diaphragm is a shallow cup with a rim that fits into the vagina over the opening to the cervix. The cervical cap is smaller and fits over the cervix itself. Both are soft pieces of rubber

182

and require the use of spermicidal cream or jelly for added protection.

↪ **Effectiveness:** Eighteen out of every 100 women who use the diaphragm will become pregnant, and thirty-six out of every 100 women who use the cervical cap will become pregnant during the first year. A woman can decrease her chances by checking that the cervix is covered each time she has intercourse. Chances can be further reduced with the careful use of spermicide before every sexual encounter.

↪ **Method:** Both the cap and the diaphragm are flexible barriers that fit over the cervix. Each device must be coated with spermicide before insertion. The diaphragm can be inserted up to six hours before intercourse and left in place for twenty-four hours. Each time intercourse is repeated, the user must apply more spermicide in the vagina without removing the diaphragm. The cervical cap may be left in place for forty-eight hours. With instruction, insertion of either device is easy and can become a part of bedtime routine. Neither partner will feel the barriers when the barriers are in position. The spermicide provides minimal protection against sexually transmitted diseases.

↪ **Cost:** The initial exam costs at least $35 and the cost for both methods is about $13 to $25 per piece. Spermicide costs about $4 to $8 per container. Medicaid and some HMOs will cover part or all of the costs. Spermicide can be obtained for free at some clinics.

↪ **Recommendation:** These methods cause no side effects, but can lead to bladder infections. These barriers must be placed correctly and must stay in position throughout intercourse to be effective. Women with poor vaginal muscle tone or a sagging uterus should not use these methods. The user should check periodically for weak spots or pinholes. The cap can be worn by most women whose pelvic muscles are too relaxed to hold a diaphragm in place. The cap may be more difficult and time-consuming to use and more difficult for the doctor to fit. However, comfort in wearing may make it preferable to the diaphragm.

↪ **Cautions:** Do not use either method while experiencing vaginal bleeding, including menstruation. Always use spermicidal cream, jelly, or foam. Have the fit checked after a full-term pregnancy, an abortion or miscarriage beyond the first three months of pregnancy, pelvic surgery, or weight loss or gain of ten or more pounds. There are no side effects unless you have an allergy to rubber, cream, or jelly or have problems with bladder infections. Report to your doctor any discomfort when the device is in place or if it does not stay in place, any irritation or itching in the genital area, frequent bladder infections, or unusual vaginal odor or discharge.

Over-the-Counter Contraceptives

Condoms (Male)

↪ **Effectiveness:** If their partners wear condoms that are used perfectly and used in combination with spermicide foam, cream, or lubricant, only three in 100 women will become pregnant during the first year of use.

↪ *Method:* The one contraceptive that is the primary responsibility of the male, the condom is a sheath of thin rubber or animal tissue worn on the penis during intercourse. Placement of the condom is important; it should be placed on the penis before any contact with the vulva. Place the rolled condom on the tip of the erect penis, pinching the air out of the half-inch at the end; then roll the condom down over the penis and smooth out any air bubbles. Remove before the penis softens by holding the rim of the condom against the penis while withdrawing from the vagina to prevent spilling of semen. The condom collects semen before, during, and after ejaculation, thus preventing sperm from entering the vagina. The condom may be purchased dry or lubricated. Only a water-based lubricant provides any protection against STDs. Condoms have no side effects except for rare allergies to rubber or spermicide. They are easily purchased by men or women and serve as a reliable back-up method. The "female condom" is also effective and stops sexually transmitted diseases. See the next section for more information.

↪ *Cost:* Condoms are available from drugstores, clinics, some supermarkets, and vending machines. Some schools and clinics provide condoms for free.

↪ *Caution*: Every condom package and individually wrapped condom comes stamped with an expiration date. Be sure to use condoms before the date that appears

185

on the box or wrapper. Do not use condoms if you cannot find any date or are unsure about their age. Men must be sure to withdraw by holding the rim of the condom against the penis to avoid spilling semen. Only latex condoms offer any protection against STDs, including AIDS. Use only a water-based lubricant. Do not use petroleum jellies or mineral or vegetable oils as a lubricant.

Over-the-Counter Birth Control for Women

Over-the-counter methods for women are reversible barrier methods. They include *contraceptive creams, foams, gels, sponges, and suppositories* and are sold as are liquids, solids, or sponges containing spermicide that are inserted into the vagina shortly before use. They are easy to use but must be replaced shortly before each use. *Vaginal pouches*, also known as *female condoms*, are available over the counter. They are polyurethane sheaths that are inserted deep into the vagina. Rings at either end help to hold the pouches in place during intercourse.

↝ *Effectiveness:* Using only one at a time (foam, cream, gel, sponges, suppositories, or vaginal pouches), twenty-one of 100 women will become pregnant during the first year of use. Using extreme care to replace liquid and solid forms of the contraceptive before each sexual encounter can reduce the chances of becoming pregnant. Many people use spermicide methods along with a male or female condom. The spermicide contained in most of these methods provides minimal protection against sexually transmitted diseases. Vaginal pouches, however, are more effective barriers against infection.

⇝ **Method:** The chemicals of the spermicide paralyze sperm but do not harm vaginal tissue. Creams, gels, and suppositories melt into a thick liquid throughout the vagina that blocks the entrance to the uterus. Sponges are soft, round, and about two inches in diameter, with a nylon loop at the bottom for easy removal. The sponge is moistened and then inserted deep into the vagina shortly before intercourse. It covers the cervix and blocks sperm from entering the uterus. While in position, it continuously releases spermicide.

⇝ **Cost:** Starter supplies of creams, foams, and gels can be purchased at most supermarkets and drugstores for about $8. Refills cost between $4 and $8, about the same price as large cans of foam containing twenty to forty applications. Suppositories are similar in price. Sponges cost $3 to $5 a package, and vaginal pouches cost about $2.50 each. Clinic prices may be more reasonable.

⇝ **Recommendation:** Foams, creams, and gels can be used by almost any woman. Sponges can be used by any woman who can use a tampon, has fingers long enough for placing and removing it, has not had toxic shock syndrome, and is not experiencing vaginal bleeding, including menstruation. Irritation of the penis or vagina by spermicide is rare and changing brands may help.

⇝ **Cautions:** As with condoms, follow time limits and expiration dates given in the instructions or on the packaging. Women must be aware of the very small possibility of contracting toxic shock syndrome. The symptoms are vomiting, high fever, diarrhea, and a sunburn-type rash.

187

Fertility Awareness Methods

Systems have been designed to help partners prevent pregnancy by remaining abstinent during certain times of each month. Kits are available to insure efficient use of these methods. Do not attempt a method without a kit. The following information should be used only as a guide in choosing a method.

Fertility awareness systems depend on the *cooperation of both partners and estimation of ovulation time.* In general, the time to abstain from intercourse is five days before and three days after an egg is released from an ovary. Four methods help the couple know when to abstain.

1. **Postovulation method**—requires that the couple abstain from vaginal intercourse from the onset of menstruation to the morning of the fourth day after estimated ovulation. This method involves more than half the menstrual cycle.

2. **Basal body temperature method**—requires taking one's temperature each morning before getting out of bed. A small but significant rise of less than one degree occurs when the egg is released and continues through menstruation. After three days of the higher temperature, the unsafe period has passed.

3. **Vaginal mucus method**—requires observing changes in vaginal moisture during the phases of the menstrual cycle. The normally tacky, cloudy mucus becomes clear and slippery and stretches between the fingers as the egg is released. When that mucus

appears, you must abstain from intercourse until four days after the last day it is observed.

4. **Calendar/rhythm method**—predicts the fertile time by tracking the menstrual cycle. It has a success rate of 70 percent.

Postpartum Emotional Changes

"Baby Blues" and Depression

On the third day after arriving home from the hospital, just as things seemed to be settling down for Min, she found herself crying for no apparent reason. Trying to stop the tears was futile. The next day she felt fine and smiled at everything her new baby did.

Nancy felt energetic and enthusiastic for the first ten days after Jamie arrived. On the third day after her husband's family left, she began to feel hopeless. The beds were not made, dishes were piled in the sink, and bottles needed to be sterilized. After three days of tears, she called her doctor.

Trisha started out blue and stayed that way. She felt unable to keep up with the work and never had time for the baby or herself. She even considered giving the baby to her sister. Her doctor noticed her sadness, irritability, and weight loss and decided that she was depressed. He prescribed rest and an antidepressant.

For many mothers, crying from the "baby blues" is limited to one episode, after which they feel much better.

189

For others, the mood may last for several months and include feelings of hopelessness, discouragement, or unnecessary worry about the baby.

Your first question is probably "Why does this happen when I should be excited about my new baby?" The answer is that the emotional ups and downs are caused by the drastic change in hormone levels, by fatigue, or by inexperience or lack of confidence with a newborn and its full-time demands. Other factors can affect your ability to beat the blues, such as the baby's temperament, your own medical complications, problems with breast-feeding, the amount of help available, and money problems. Your expectations of yourself may be too high and you may be inflexible when things go wrong or change.

Help Yourself Through the Baby Blues

Start by forgiving yourself for such things as dirty dishes or an unmade bed, then remind yourself that you are doing the best you can. And if you feel like crying . . . go ahead and do it.

Take time for yourself. Set aside at least fifteen minutes twice a day or as much as two hours if possible. Plan one activity a week just for you—a community activity, aerobics, or a trip to the library. Keep from being totally swallowed up by the needs of the family.

Make adult contacts. Talk with an adult every day by visiting in person or by telephone; include both parents and nonparents. Vent your feelings to a friend. Call your best friend. Talk to a social worker or a counselor.

Go on outings with family or friends.

Stay informed and keep your mind active by listening to

the news, reading the newspaper, or joining or forming a book discussion group. Read or listen to taped books.

Join support groups to get and share information and advice on parenting issues.

Avoid caffeine and sugar, which cause mood swings, especially in the afternoon and evening when you are less stable.

Stay busy. Make a "to do" list for the day even if it only includes your usual activities. Cross them off as you finish.

Set a time to spend outdoors and stick to it. Baby can be taken along.

If the blues do not go away but just seem to get worse, and you find yourself worrying about little things, use the following list of symptoms to check your feelings. If you experience these more severe symptoms of the blues beginning about two weeks after delivery, call your doctor. The more severe change of mood is depression. Watch for:

- crying spells; a change in sleep patterns; loss of appetite

- a feeling of hopelessness just short of despair (inability to experience any pleasure; thoughts of death or suicide)

- feelings of failure day and night

- fatigue that makes you feel weighed down or an inability to cope with day-to-day responsibilities

- excessive talking or unnecessary worrying; terrifying anxieties

- feelings of restlessness, irritability, or a need for isolation

- hostile feelings toward baby or a loss of interest in yourself, your baby, and your family

- difficultly concentrating, remembering, and making decisions

Treatment

Depression, which occurs in 10 percent of new mothers, can be successfully treated with antidepressant medication or therapy. Only occasionally is hospitalization needed. If you have a prior history of problems or if there are signs of depression during pregnancy, the doctor may take preventive steps. Hormones may be given immediately after delivery or an antidepressant and therapy prescribed for the early postpartum period. *A major key to recovery from a depression is family support.*

Parent Care:
Your Own Needs

Your life has changed! A new world has opened up requiring you to make many sacrifices. Meeting your obligations as a parent has redirected your use of time, energy, and money. Your activities now revolve around the financial responsibilities and physical labor of taking care of someone else. That someone, your baby, depends on you for every need. The baby will feel secure when his or her calls are answered consistently with love and warmth. You may feel some frustration at being called on so often. The frustration or anger you feel may be a reaction to the changes in your freedom. You can no longer come and go easily or whenever you want. You may not always have time for both your needs and the baby's. The energy it takes to care for the baby really drains you.

These feelings are normal. It is how you deal with them that is important. Even when you are angry or frustrated, you must think of your baby's need for stability. Your reactions to your baby's frequent calls must be met without your frustrations showing. The baby is not responsible for your loss of freedom, and he or she should not have to pay for that loss. For your child to feel secure, you must not allow your feelings to change how you meet his or her needs. If your feelings are strong, you must be careful that they do not cause you to abuse your child. Ask for help with the baby and your feelings. Talk to someone immediately—your parent(s), a doctor, a school counselor, or a social worker.

Take Care of Yourself

Your mental and physical health are important. You must feel healthy and feel good about yourself. You can improve your self-concept and your physical well-being in four ways:

1. ***Do not give up the things you enjoy doing unless they are bad for your health or well-being.*** Find time for exercise, sunshine, and fun with and without the baby. Practice good nutrition. Get plenty of rest.

2. ***Keep your goals in life and be the parent you want to be.*** Plans for your education or career may have been changed at least temporarily. If it is necessary for you to work, you must divide your time between the baby, your job, and you. You may have taken a job that is convenient instead of embarking upon the career you always wanted. You may have had to quit school to care for the baby or to make money. Do not give up your dreams. You can be the kind of parent you want to be and accomplish your life goals with careful planning. How? Chapter sixteen will guide you in planning a realistic timeline to meet your life goals.

   As a parent, keep in mind that it is not always the amount of time you spend with your child but the quality of the time that makes a difference. Plan fun, learning, and loving activities with your child. Find ways to include your child as you take care of household tasks, study, read, and have fun. You can talk to your baby while you fold clothes, wash dishes, or shine your shoes. You may find that you can entertain your baby and learn at the same time by reading your assignments aloud. With an occasional smile and a gentle touch, your baby can be shown the love and warmth he or she needs to grow up emotionally healthy. The two of you will learn together. He or she will have the opportunity to hear language and the rhythm of reading, and you will be prepared for class.

3. **Find the private time you need.** Parenting, school, spouse, baby needs, household chores . . . what about the other things that interest you? Are you having to give up reading for fun, tennis, or visiting friends? What about your private or quiet time and personal care? Keeping yourself well-groomed helps you feel good about yourself. How do you find time for your yourself? Where do you find this time?

Parenting and childcare must be shared. If you are a single parent, special arrangements may need to be made. If you live with your parents, friends, or relatives, talk to them about scheduling a regular time for you to get away. Also be willing to let them know when your frustrations are building. A walk around the block may be all you need. Another possibility is to trade relief time with a friend who has a child. Always choose someone you trust to follow your expectations for your child's care. Make sure that anyone, relative or friend, you leave your child with can be trusted. If you have reason to believe that someone may abuse or neglect your child, never allow that person to be alone with your child. You are the parent, the protector of your child.

Don't forget that both mothers and fathers should participate in parenting. Fathers are sometimes overlooked as sources of love, care, and guidance for the baby. Fathers are needed sooner than being there to throw the first ball or to "check out" a daughter's first boyfriend; they should be included in all aspects of parenting from the very beginning. Learn childcare together; a child benefits from the double share of warmth and love.

In some situations, a parent may need to use a mother's-day-out program. A carefully chosen day care arrangement will give you both needed relief time. Time away can be beneficial for both parent and child. Not only do you come back to your child rested and refreshed, but your child has the opportunity to be with other children and to learn to relate to other adults.

4. **Plan family-style entertainment.** Outings or trips that include the child can be successful and enjoyed by all with careful planning. Taking the baby along eliminates the worry of how he or she is doing while you are out; allows you to go when you want; and eliminates babysitting costs.

Plan Ahead for Outings

Try one- to three-hour outings before planning a day-long outing or overnight trip. You will want to avoid having to purchase items just because you forgot to pack them. A hungry or wet baby whose needs cannot be met is going to be unhappy. Not being able to take care of your baby can turn a wonderful outing into a disaster for everyone. Plan ahead. By the time you're ready for an outing with the baby, you may be aware of all the items needed for the care and comfort of him or her. If you aren't sure of what or how much to take, make a list of all baby-care items used in one hour, three hours, or one day, or set aside baby-care items as you use them and count the number used in a given period. Add extras to be sure. Take at least two changes of clothing for the baby for any outing and at least three changes of clothing for baby for a day-long excursion. On an extended trip, you may have to go to a laundromat. Dress yourself for comfort and take a change of clothing in case of baby spit-ups or spills.

Free and Inexpensive Entertainment/ Outings for Parents

⇨ *With baby*
   picnics
   parks
   playgrounds
   zoos or botanical gardens
   outdoor family concerts

seasonal activities such as fireworks shows, holiday displays, fairs

special shows presented in shopping malls

➥ *Without baby*

parks-YMCA softball, volleyball, etc. (informal or league)

movies—special price matinees

museums

community schools (calligraphy, painting and drawing, sports, cooking, exercise, and computer classes; school plays; debates; football games)

Think and Talk About

Special Obstacles for Teen Parents Regarding Self-Care

You have read in chapter one and at the end of the other chapters about the five obstacles that teen parents face. Choose one or two areas that you feel make your life more difficult. Then turn to chapter fifteen and start planning to overcome them.

Financial Planning for Now and the Future

Because of your age and lack of education, experience, or available childcare, you may have to depend on one or more of the following for support: family members, welfare, a part-time job, a low-paying full-time job, or more than one job. If you are old enough to hold a job and have a high school diploma or know a trade or skill, you may be supporting your new family. You may need little outside support. Only unexpected expenses like illness or a high utility bill may cause financial problems. If you are continuing to pursue an education, you may need help with the added expenses of getting to and from school or college, buying books and supplies, and paying tuition.

Since you are just beginning as a parent and provider, you should not measure your success by where or how you get support. Comparing what you have to what others have is also not a good measure of how you are doing. Each person's situation is different. You measure success by what you do with what you have. You may not have large amounts of money or possessions. Your success comes from using what you have wisely. Available money is used to meet your family's needs first and its "wants" second. Needs of the baby come before those of the parents. Yes, diapers and formula come before entertainment. School and work clothes come before a new bathing suit. . . .

Then how do you measure your ability to handle your money and your obligations? Measure your success in three ways. First, measure by how well you manage the money you do have. If the basic needs of your new family come first on your list, you are doing a good job. Second, measure by how often you take extra jobs to meet and save for the unexpected. When someone offers you a temporary babysitting job, you take it. Your aunt has a room to paint; you do the job in your spare time. Whether you need extra money for basic family needs, saving for the future or emergencies, or to have a little money for entertainment, you go for it. Third, measure by your life goals. You believe the pursuit of your life goals is important. You are using your family's support or welfare as stepping-stones to becoming a successful provider for your family. You are taking every opportunity to finish your education or learn a trade or skill. Each step toward your dreams—finishing high school, starting college, learning a trade—is a step closer to the maturity, freedom, and satisfaction that come with being an independent, self-supporting adult. You take each step with pride.

Think and Talk About

Some families with two working adults in high-paying jobs are not successful. They struggle from week to week or month to month to make ends meet because of what they do with what they have. Family needs may come second to wants. They may purchase a luxury item to get temporary satisfaction and leave a bill unpaid. The priorities of food, clothing, or shelter come second.

"I have to be able to surprise my daughters with gifts once in a while," thinks Jackie as she hands a $20 bill to the store cashier. Giving little presents to her children is important to the nineteen-year-old mom of two. "It's a part of making both of them feel better, since they don't have a daddy," Jackie adds to herself. She tries to be careful about buying too many "extras," but as she walks to her car she remembers that the end of the month is fast approaching and her rent check will once again be due. With regret she turns around and goes back to the store to return the items she bought only a few minutes before.

"When I had my first child and started receiving welfare, it was tough to make ends meet," remembers Jackie. "I always wanted to take a course to learn to become a travel agent, but just catching up and then taking care of Belle was too much. When I got pregnant again, I thought, 'Good, now I'll get more help from welfare for my second child.' I planned how I would use the extra couple of hundred each month: buy a new suit, finally get that computer, and maybe even take my kids on a trip." But after her Temporary Assistance to Needy Families (TANF) benefit was adjusted, the difference quickly disappeared. At first she didn't notice because of the help she received from friends. But in a few months she realized that the second baby created many new expenses. And now, a year after her second child arrived, it is even more difficult to think about starting work again.

Look to the Future

If you are a parent, you hold the future of a new family in your hands. Your day-to-day buying decisions and the step-by-step struggle you make toward meeting your life goals are your investment in that future. The rewards come from meeting daily needs and steadily gaining on your life goals. Weekly purchases of unnecessary items might make you feel good for a while, but the spending sprees could add up to a delay in your dreams—paid bills, your own car, a home in the future. You need to: (1) budget for necessities—items like diapers and groceries; (2) plan ahead for the expected—a rent deposit on your own place in three months, or this month's rent; (3) plan ahead for the unexpected, such as having to take clothes out to the laundromat because of a broken washer or an illness that keeps you from working; and (4) save for or at least look ahead to the major needs and wants of the future—a stroller for baby, a new coat for the winter, or a down payment on a car.

A Budget to Live By

What is budgeting? It is allocating (setting aside) parts of your income to cover your expenses. It is a way of estimating (carefully guessing) the amount of money you will have and planning for its use for family needs. A budget is made to cover a given period of time—a week, a month, a year. Budgeting makes you establish goals. The goals are set to keep or improve your lifestyle and to meet your obligations. The record-keeping that budgeting requires should help in three ways: (1) It will keep you from running out of money before more money arrives; (2) it will allow you set to aside money for necessities; and (3) it will let you see your spending habits. With a written budget you will know:

⮞ where your money is coming from

⮞ where your money is going

⮞ how much money you have used in a given period

⮞ future money needs

⮞ the need to be more careful with the money received

⮞ the need to control your spending (financial self-discipline)

⮞ the information needed to solve family money arguments

⮞ which spending habits must be changed to live within your income

⮞ how to save for the more expensive needs—car, home, etc.

Think . . . Talk . . . Design a Budget

All family and money situations are different. Sample budgets cannot be given for every possibility. The following sample is given to show you a budget that worked. It also will help you in setting yours up in a similar format. Look at the budget for Jan and Jon Jones for the month of December. Think about your situation and plan a written budget.

A typical family budget plans ahead six to twelve months. If circumstances change, adjustments must be made. If you work or receive welfare payments, your budget period will depend on whether you receive payments weekly or monthly. Each budget period should be short enough to eliminate as much guesswork as possible. (If your money comes from parents, as needed, your budget will be a guide for them as to your future needs each month.) When large expenses such as rent or house payments must come from several weekly pay periods in the month, you should budget a portion of the money each week.

A SAMPLE BUDGET

Names: <u>Jan and Jon Jones</u>   Children: James—1 month
        2929 Not-So-Easy St.   Jan—1 year
        Hometown, NY 29098

Date: <u>Dec.1</u>

OBLIGATIONS/NEEDS	Budgeted	Actual
Rent	225.00	225.00
Utilities		
Electricity	60.00	48.50
Water	15.00	12.60
Food (includes at-home, take-out, eating out, and snack items)	200.00	205.09

Clothing and laundry	25.00	0.00
Transportation (bus)	25.00	17.50
Medical and dental	35.00	0.00
Household supplies	10.00	5.25
Grooming supplies	10.00	15.40
School		
Tuition	435.00	485.00
Books	50.00	75.82
Savings	25.00	25.00
Holiday expenses	<u>50.00</u>	<u>53.84</u>
	1165.00	1170.00

INCOME AND SOURCES:

Salary (Jon)	486.00
Jon (painting for Pat)	50.00
Jan (baby-sitting)	200.00
Parents (tuition)	<u>435.00</u>
	1171.00

What did you notice in the sample budget?

1. Costs for electricity and water change from month to month. The costs were estimated (good guesses were made based on previous months).

2. Even though it was holiday season, Jon and Jan stuck to their budget. (Their regular $25 a month was placed in their savings account. Emergency money for the year will total more than $300 because of regular savings and any leftover money each month.)

3. Expenses for the next semester of college for Jan were planned and allocated. The amount of money in their budget is higher this month because of Jan's parents' addition of tuition costs.

4. Jan's mother keeps the children while Jan is in school. Jan watches one child for a friend who works in the evenings.

5. Jon took a painting job for a friend during his spare time. The money was allocated through budgeting. They accounted for all funds.

6. Holiday spending was limited to the extra money from the painting job.

7. Because of the books and supplies needed by Jan, no clothing was purchased during the month.

8. If the family had needed medical or dental care in December, they would have had to reduce holiday spending or their savings. With their savings plan, they are preparing for the unexpected.

Your Budget

List each of the following that applies to you. Make sure all of the needs, including savings, are met in your budget before adding wants. Your budget must balance. Your expenses (money spent) cannot be larger than income (money coming in).

NEEDS
Fixed Expenses
Housing
  (rent, mortgage
  payments, etc.)
Utilities
  (gas, electricity, etc.)
Food
Clothing and laundry
Transportation
Medical and dental
Debt repayment (loans)
Household supplies
Grooming supplies
Insurance
School expenses (tuition,
  books, supplies, etc.)
Savings for emergencies/
  future needs and wants
TOTAL:

SOURCES OF INCOME
  Job(s)
  TANF/welfare
  Food stamps
  Other
TOTAL:

WANTS
Changing Expenses
Travel, vacations, etc.
Recreation and
  entertainment
Books, magazines, movies,
  etc.
Gifts
Household furnishings
Other

Living with a Budget

Becoming a parent presents challenges. The additional demands of the baby on your time, energy, and money may cause frustration. It is not easy to feed another mouth. It is not painless to give up or postpone your lifelong dreams. Living with a budget can be difficult and tiring. Doing without your "wants" may make you feel blue. Not having enough money to meet the budget can cause frustration. To feel good during these beginning tough times, try hard to meet the budget. And continue to dream and work toward your life goals and the career you desire.

Think and Talk About

Special Obstacles for Teen Parents Concerning Finances

↪ *A limited number of people are available to share the responsibility of parenting with the teen parent.* Teen parents must find ways of providing care for their baby or child if they want to continue school or work. (See chapter eleven for suggestions.)

↪ *Teen parents are in the adolescent stage of growth and development.* Teens must be able to accept financial help and still see their path toward independence. Part of the maturing process is accepting help—including money, love, and guidance—from parents and keeping a good feeling about who you are becoming. If a teen is receiving help to reach for higher goals, he or she will feel better about himself or herself—better about what he or she wants to do and to be. The relationship with parents and other adults can grow.

↪ *Fertility levels of teen parents are higher than those of other groups.* The younger the parent, the more children he or she is likely to have in less time. A teen striving to meet the needs of a new family and to become independent needs to be aware of the added expenses each additional child will bring. Teens can get free or inexpensive help in planning their families. Family doctors, most clinics, and Planned Parenthood agencies are willing to help.

☛ *Life plans change or are postponed.* Many young people return to high school. College is not just for recent high school graduates. Returning to school may take some sacrifices, but the idea must not be abandoned. Share baby-sitting with someone else. Finish high school. It is the job of high school counselors to help you. College admission offices and student aid offices exist to help students with entry requirements and to help you find the resources to attend. Do not be afraid to ask for help. Your dreams and future are at stake.

☛ *Family structure and lifestyles change.* Teen parents may have to live at home temporarily and receive support from their parents or welfare. But that too can be temporary. People's lives and lifestyles can change many times. In the past you were Mom's and Dad's little one. Only last year you were a student concerned only about french fries, homework, and dates. Today you are a teen parent living at home concerned about formula and diapers. Tomorrow, with the continued pursuit of your dreams, you may be a high school graduate, a college student with a child at home, a nurse, a welder with a special skill, or a renter or homeowner. In the future you may be the parent of a student, football player, teen parent, or college graduate—you hold the key. Keep the key turning toward your life dreams. Work with those who are providing for you and your child now. Continue to look for and ask about every opportunity available to help you establish your independence: school, college, special job skills.

Planning Your Life Goals

The setting of life goals is very important to your feelings about yourself and to your ultimate success in life. Your goals will be ever-changing as your situation changes. When you reach a goal, you can see the next higher goals that can be set and reached. If you have not finished high school, college may seem very far away. Each goal you meet takes you one step closer. You gain the power from one success to see farther and higher.

This chapter could be a blank page for you to write out your life goals. However, a sample set of goals and a format may be helpful in getting you started. Fill out this page willingly and with hope for your future. Build bridges, climb mountains, and do a thousand other things that will bring achievement and satisfaction. See every small step as a giant leap toward who you will be as an adult. Setting and meeting future goals is important to you and to your child.

Think and Talk About

The following is an example of one young woman's on-going life goal plan. Look it over before you start planning your life goals. Your situation may not be similar. You may not have many of the same life goals. Nevertheless, you can use her plan to get you thinking. Notice such things as the time she took off from school for the birth of a child. Her marriage came earlier than the date set. She did return to high school and get her diploma. She shows that college will take more than four years because she cannot take a full load. She is being realistic. The record of the plan will become a diary of her success.

Set Goals, then Reset Goals When Obstacles Get in the Way

Goal	Date Set	Reset Date	Goal Achieved
Complete high school	5/96	1/97	1/97
Get married	5/99		5/96
Learn about child care	11/96		Ongoing
Lose ten pounds after baby	12/96	2/97	9/97
Start college	9/96	9/97	9/97
Get an apartment	9/96	9/98	9/98
Complete freshman year	12/98		
Finish college	5/02		
Get a job as a teacher	9/02		
Plan for a second child	12/02		

Now it's Your Turn! Use the form by checking off the goals that apply to you. Cross out the others. Add your own. Set realistic dates for completion. Do not hesitate to change dates if your situation changes. You may even complete some goals early.

Goal	Date Set	Reset Date	Steps to Success*	Goal Achieved
Finish high school				
Start college				
Finish college				
Get an apartment				
Get a job				
Learn about parenting skills				
Read about nutrition and change the way my family eats				
Take care of myself, exercise, find time to regroup				

*To reach a goal, steps must be taken. If you plan to enter college, you must apply and be accepted, get a catalog and an adviser to plan your beginning classes, apply for a loan or scholarship, etc. Use this space to list all the steps necessary to the success of your goal. Check off each step as you complete it.

Where to Find Information

Teen parents can find information in a number of ways. Listed below is information about publications you can obtain concerning health, nutrition, medical concerns, and other aspects of parenting. Also included is information on obtaining a Social Security number for your child.

Free Pamphlets

The next time you take your child to the doctor or clinic, look around the waiting room for free pamphlets on child rearing. You usually can find pamphlets on a variety of topics, including breast-feeding, nutrition, and toilet-training. Feel free to take any of the information offered.

Government Publications

You can obtain a set of ten free books known as the "Help Your Child Series" from the U.S. Department of Education. These books address all issues from infancy to late childhood about helping to educate your child. Call or write:

Department of Education
Attn: Publications
555 New Jersey Avenue, NW
Washington, DC 20208–5641
(202) 219-2050 (If you are calling, ask for publications.)

In addition, a wide range of materials, both books and pamphlets, are available from the U.S. Government Printing Office. They address issues of interest to teen parents, such as child care, nutrition, health, and finances. The cost for these materials ranges from $1 to $40 for some of the books, including shipping and handling. A complete list of the available publications, listed by topic, is featured in the Index of Publications. To receive a copy of this index, either call and request a copy or send your name, address, and a request for the Index of Publications to:

Superintendent of Documents
P. O. Box 371954
Pittsburgh, PA 15250–7954
(202) 512-1800

The following publication from the U.S. Government Printing Office may be of particular interest to teen parents. Use the above address to order. (Price includes shipping and handling.)

The First Aid Book.
S/N 024-017-00006-9 $16
Fully illustrated manual with basic first-aid techniques for dealing with common accidents and injuries.

Helpful Books

Additional books that may be extremely helpful to teen parents include:

Arthur, Shirley M. *Surviving Teen Pregnancy: Your Choices, Dreams, and Decisions.* Buena Park, CA: Morning Glory Press, 1996.

Boston Women's Health Book Collective. *The New Our Bodies, Ourselves.* New York: Touchstone, 1992.

Brown, Deni. *Healthy Pregnancy.* New York: D K Publishing, 1997.

Edelson, Paula. *Straight Talk About Teenage Pregnancy.* New York: Facts on File, 1998.

Eisenberg, Arlene, Heide E. Murkoff, and Sandee E. Hathaway. *What to Expect the First Year.* 3rd ed. New York: Workman Publishers, 1996. Extremely thorough and helpful book that answers almost every question about your baby from birth until the child is one year old.

Englander, Annrenee. *Dear Diary, I'm Pregnant: Teenagers Talk About Their Pregnancy.* Buffalo, NY: Firefly Books, 1997.

Fields, Denise. *Baby Bargains.* Boulder, CO: Windsor Peak Press, 1997. A guide for saving money through thrifty parenting as your baby grows.

Iovine, Vicki. *The Girlfriends Guide to Pregnancy.* Garden City, NY: Doubleday Direct, 1997.

La Leche League International. *The Womanly Art of Breastfeeding.* New York: Plume Books, New American Library, 1997. This book addresses everything a nursing mother needs to know about breast-feeding.

Lindsay, Jeanne W. *Teen Dads: Rights, Responsibilities,*

and Joys. Buena Park, CA: Morning Glory
Press, 1997.

Moglia, Ronald Filiberti, and Jon Knowles. *All About
Sex: A Family Resource on Sex and Sexuality.*
New York: Crown Publishers, 1997.

Stewart, Deborah D. *Baby and Me: The Essential Guide
to Pregnancy.* 3rd ed. Lake Forest Park, WA:
Willapa Bay Co., 1998.

Stewart, Gail. *Teen Fathers.* San Diego: Lucent
Books, 1997.

Subak-Sharpe, Genell J., ed. *Columbia University
College of Physicians and Surgeons Complete
Guide to Early Child Care.* New York: Crown
Publishers, 1990. Wonderfully comprehensive
book that addresses questions about your child's
physical and emotional health and development,
from newborn through toddler.

Trapani, Marge. *Listen Up: Teenage Mothers Speak
Out.* 8 vols. New York: Rosen Publishing Group,
1997.

Helpful Web sites

http://www.cfoc.org—Campaign for Our Children (CFOC)
uses this site to list statistics about the development and
condition of children in the United States. Look for the
clock, a tabulation of teen births each year, and chat rooms,
where teens can exchange advice about growing up.

http://www.plannedparenthood.org—a great resource for
information on birth control, dating, relationships, and teen
pregnancy. The Planned Parenthood Federation of Canada
also has its own Web site, **http://www.ppfc.org**.

217

http://www.parentsoup.com—this site, which includes chat rooms for parents, tips, and message boards, is a good place to have specific questions answered.

http://www.teenshelter.org—a California-based residential home for teens that offers links on teen pregnancy and stories from real teen moms. Also has information on adoption, prenatal care, and where to get help.

Other Publications

Planned Parenthood can help you find information on topics ranging from birth control to health issues concerning pregnancy and sex. To obtain a free catalog of Planned Parenthood's current publications, write or call:

Planned Parenthood
Attn: Marketing Department
810 Seventh Avenue
New York, NY 10019
(212) 541-7800

Postpartum Support, International provides information for parents concerning the mood changes, especially depression and anxiety, that can occur in a mother after giving birth. Write or call:

Postpartum Support, International
927 North Kellogg Avenue
Santa Barbara, CA 93111
(805) 967-7636

The Postpartum Mood Disorders Clinic specializes in and treats mothers suffering from the mood changes, especially depression and anxiety, that can occur after giving birth. Contact it at:

Postpartum Health Alliance
P.O. Box 503396
San Diego, CA 92150-3396
(619) 685-7458

Obtaining a Social Security Number for Your Child

Federal law requires Social Security cards for children one or more years old who will be counted as dependents on a parent's tax return. This procedure generally is completed at the hospital itself. The hospital will provide you with a form (ask for it if they don't give it to you before you leave) that requires your name, the father's name, your occupation, the child's name, your mother's maiden name (for security purposes), and answers to other routine questions. Be sure to fill out the form completely and to return it to the hospital. In about six to eight weeks you should receive the child's birth certificate in the mail. The child's Social Security card will follow, about six months after the day the child was born.

If you did not complete the form in the hospital, call to request forms or information. Call (800) 772-1213 for Social Security #5. An official copy of the child's birth certificate and your identification are needed to complete the application. When the process is complete, your child's Social Security card will be sent to you.

Ignore direct-mail solicitations from firms offering to complete the process for a fee. They are not governmental organizations. You will save time and money by completing it yourself.

Caution: Some parenting magazines and other sources offer child care and women's information by telephone. Check the fee. Many of the information lines are expensive to use.

Where to Find Help

Learning to ask for help is a crucial part of growing up and adapting to changes in your life. Many people believe that asking for help is a sign of failure and weakness. This is absolutely untrue. At some point in their lives, all people have turned to others for help. In the United States and Canada, many facilities and telephone information lines exist, most of which are available to help you twenty-four hours a day. Hotlines allow you to keep your anonymity as you speak honestly and obtain useful suggestions. Remember that helping yourself and your child can only make things smoother and more pleasant for you. If you call an agency or hotline and they cannot give you an immediate response, they will be able to guide you to the next best solution. Reach out to someone when you're in trouble.

Following are a number of hotlines and organizations that may be helpful to you.

Family Services Hotlines

Boys Town Hotline   **(800) 448-3000**
       en Español   **(800) 448-3000**
Web site: http://www.ffbh.boystown.org
This hotline has trained counselors who can help you if

you are abusing your child. Referrals are provided twenty-four hours a day, seven days a week.

Childhelp USA   (800) 4-A-CHILD (422-4453)
Web site: http://www.childhelp.org
This hotline has trained counselors who can help you if you are abusing your child or if your child is being abused by someone else. Referrals are provided twenty-four hours a day, seven days a week.

Children's Rights of America Youth Crisis Hotline/
  Abuse Report Hotline   (800) 442-HOPE
500 Sugar Mill Road
Building B, Suite 220
Atlanta, GA 30350

Domestic Violence Hotline   (800) 942-6906
          en Español   (800) 942-6908
This hotline provides counselors who can help you if you are being abused by your spouse/girlfriend/boyfriend or if you are abusive toward your spouse/girlfriend/boyfriend. Referrals are made twenty-four hours a day, seven days a week.

Giratto Institute/Parents
  United Parental Stress Hotline   (408) 453-7616
232 East Gish Road
San Jose, CA 95112
This organization assists parents who want to stop sexually abusing their children. Call the hotline to speak to a

counselor or call the main number for referral to support groups in your area. This institute also serves child and adult victims of sexual abuse.

National Domestic Violence Hotline   **(800) 749-SAFE**

National Runaway Switchboard   **(800) 621-4000**
Web site: http://www.nrscrisis.org

Parents Anonymous   **(909) 621-6184**
Parents Anonymous is a self-help support group for parents—married or unmarried couples, single parents, teen parents, grandparents—who are overwhelmed by raising children and want to learn better ways of coping. It is free of charge. The Parents Anonymous headquarters helps parents learn techniques for coping with and avoiding physical and emotional abuse. Call the number above for referrals to local Parents Anonymous groups for parents and children. (8:00 AM to 4:30 PM Pacific Standard Time)

Youth Crisis and Runaway Hotline   **(800) 448-4663**
Trained counselors on this hotline can help you in times of crisis. Referrals are provided twenty-four hours a day, seven days a week.

Health Lines

Birth Right Hotline   **(800) 550-4900**
Help for pregnant women.

**CDC National STD (Sexually Transmitted
Diseases) Hotline**   **(800) 227-8966**

Lead Poisoning Hotline   **(800) LEAD-FYI (532-3394)**
                             (800) 424-LEAD (424-5323)
An information hotline about lead and lead poisoning and ways of minimizing exposure.

National Health Information Center   **(800) 336-4797**
                 (In Maryland: (301) 565-4167)
A telephone network service provided by the National Health Information Center can refer you to more than 1,000 public service organizations that have tollfree numbers, brochures, or programs for handling various health problems. No diagnosis or treatment will be given over the phone. Health topics available are as varied as nutrition and exercise, stress, and cancer.

Aerobics and Fitness Foundation........(800) YOUR-BODY

AIDS.....................................(800) 342-AIDS

PMS Access....................(800) 222-4767

(in Wisconsin, (800) 833-4767)

Pregnancy: ASPO/Lamaze..........(800) 368-4404

Other Family Service Numbers

American Association for
  Marriage and Family Therapy   **(800) 374-2638**
Provides a list of qualified professionals in your area.

National Information Center for Children
  and Youth with Disabilities   **(800) 999-5599**
Provides free information to assist parents in helping children with disabilities become participating community members.

**National Organization
for Victims' Assistance**   **(202) 232-6682**
This group promotes the rights of victims, including assaulted children.

The National Self-Help Clearinghouse   **(212) 354-8525**
A place for finding a variety of self-help resources.

New Life Family Services   **(888) 690-HOPE**
Offers adoption services, abortion alternatives, information on abstinence, and support for single mothers, infertile couples, and women who have had abortions.

Postpartum Health Alliance   **(619) 685-7458**

Single Parent Resource Center   **(212) 951-7030**
Provides resources for one-parent families.

Victims of Crime Resource Center   **(800) 627-6872**
Provides information for survivors of crime.

In Canada

Astra Program   **(604) 951-4821**
Nisha Family and Children's Services Society
Suite 3
10318 East Whalley Ring Road
Surrey, BC V5C 5E9

225

Planned Parenthood
   Federation of Canada   **(613) 241-4474**
Web site: http://www.ppfc.ca
1 Nicholas Street, Suite 430
Ottawa, ON K1N 7B7

Pregnancy Outreach Program   **(604) 299-9731**
Burnaby Family Life Institute
32-250 Willingdon Avenue
Burnaby, BC V5C 5E9

Index